MY DREAM FROM IRELAND TO AMERICA

MY DREAM FROM IRELAND TO AMERICA

Please Call Me Sheila

Sheila O'Sullivan Becker

iUniverse, Inc.
New York Lincoln Shanghai

MY DREAM FROM IRELAND TO AMERICA
Please Call Me Sheila

iUniverse books may be ordered through booksellers or by contacting:

iUniverse
2021 Pine Lake Road, Suite 100
Lincoln, NE 68512
www.iuniverse.com
1-800-Authors (1-800-288-4677)

ISBN-13: 978-0-595-38318-4 (pbk)
ISBN-13: 978-0-595-82690-2 (ebk)
ISBN 10: 0 595 38318 1 (pbk)
ISBN-10: 0-595-82690-3 (ebk)

Printed in the United States of America

MY DREAM FROM IRELAND TO AMERICA

PLEASE CALL ME SHEILA

MY DREAM FROM IRELAND TO AMERICA

By Sheila O'Sullivan Becker

February 2002

Dedicated to my two grandchildren Julie Ann and Jennifer Rene' Washabaugh.

CHAPTER I

MY DREAM FROM IRELAND TO AMERICA

I was born in Claraghatlea, Millstreet, County Cork, Ireland on June 28, 1927. One of seventeen children born to Cornelius and Mary O' Sullivan (nee Meaney), I was number eight and learned early in life to fight for survival, both emotionally and physically. My father was the son of a school teacher who was called," Con (Cornelius) the Schoolmaster". This title carried on to him, but in reality he was a farmer and never taught a day in his life. He was a tall good-looking man. Regarding my mother, for many years I thought she was an only child, but only recently learned that she had a half brother whom I know nothing about to this day. Growing up in a small thatched roof house, with-

I was born in the house on the left. The house on the right is new.

out toilet facilities, in the countryside of Ireland had its advantages and disadvantages. I will dismiss for now any discussion of the disadvantages, some of which must be obvious. On the plus side I had the ability to choose favorite sisters and brothers; to have the freedom to climb Mount Clara, and walk our 70 acres of land and beyond.

My dad and uncle Patrick who lived with us were responsible for the care and feeding of the animals. Father was responsible for buying and selling animals, which included cows, horses, pigs, donkeys, and various fowl. The fowl consisted of chickens, geese, and turkeys.

Calves were taken to a special area in the farm where none of the other farm animals could harm them. These calves were fed twice daily, and of course had the run of many acres of land. All animals on the farm were medically taken

Left to right: Brother Denny, Dad, Uncle Pad, Sister Peg with Child. Mother is sitting.

care of by our town veterinarian. Then when the calves matured a decision was made to either sell them or keep them on the farm. This happened about four times a year when a fair was organized in the town of Millstreet a short distance from our home. That is when my dad would take his animals to the fair to be sold.

When my dad did not return home with the animals he took, then it was taken for granted that he had good luck with the sale of his animals.

Our house was located in a lovely, picturesque area amid lots of trees, with the gorgeous Clara Mountain in the background. All of us had to work very hard, and many times my back ached from weeding vegetables, turning turf, which was used in place of coal for heat in the winter, and cooking our meals on a wide open fire all year. Needless to say we never went hungry, as there was plenty of

1977—I'm with Nephew Jerry Kelleher and Deny.

produce and livestock. Our meals were filling but uneventful except for certain holidays during the year and on Sundays. Concerning Sundays, they were the only days we had for play, and I took full advantage of them by always playing out doors and taking long walks.

This was also my escape mechanism. I still remember my Mother singing constantly as she had a baby in her lap or arms. Her songs were sad and quite often in Gaelic reflecting or referencing to the brutal English invasion and the subsequent oppressive rules the Irish endured for many years.

As mentioned she was an only daughter, with one stepbrother whom I never met, nor did she ever mention his name. She was a tall slender lady who worked very hard, and was pregnant 22 times. I often recall how much her life changed when she married my dad, as she lived in a house in the town of Millstreet. In a house with all the modern day conveniences and, by that I mean indoor toilets, electric lights, decent beds etc. My mother gave up all these conveniences when she married my dad. I am sure way back then even if she was unhappy she was not allowed to express her feelings. She had to

1963—Daughters Meg & Kit at Denny's Farm.

follow the teachings of the Catholic Church, which taught one to endure and persevere. Although I had 16 brothers and sisters, I never met the other 5 as they died either in infancy or before age 2. My mom endured a great number of hardships, working from early morning until late at night. Her

dress attire was dismal. She wore an apron made of material that the oats would come in and this was like burlap or some very course cotton. She did all her own sewing.

I will always remember giving my home address to a colleague of mine, when I was a student nurse in England. She lived about 15 miles from my home. She did go and visit my parents. However when she returned to England she informed all my colleagues that my mom had two different shoes on. That really hurt my feelings, as I was ashamed that the other students would find out about this.

Mom and Dad, taken at sister Kate's Wedding to Tadhg O'Driscoll. Peggy in the back.

New home Millstreet, County Cork Ireland.

My mom wore different shoes because she did not own a pair without holes. However she did own a long black coat, which was given to her when she was about 55 years old. A doctor's wife in the town where we lived gave this to her. Mom also wore a hat with this coat, given to her by a friend. She looked elegant in this coat and hat. Looking back, I realize she had so few pleasures in life.

OPEN SPACES

I recall with joy the Sundays I would go up the mountains with my brothers and sisters and take a bucket, or some kind of a container, where we would spend hours picking either gooseberries, black currants, or any wild fruits. Also on the way home, we would pick apples from someone's orchard, bring-

In Millstreet. Kate's wedding. Left to right: Tadhg, Kate, Deny, Peg and Brother Pat in back

ing our pickings to mom who would make the most delicious pies and apple cakes. This was usually done on Sunday afternoon, as that was the only time we were free from work on the farm. The weather was usually nice then, and I was able to enjoy those few hours away from slavery, by having fun with my brothers and sisters.

We took the dogs with us on our berry picking adventures. They sensed when we were getting ready to go out into the fields and became as excited as us. Of course they spent their time running around the fields. At the base of Clara Mountain ran a stream along a ditch and here we spent a great deal of time watching all kinds of nature in action. There were bugs, insects and tiny animals, sheltered in overgrown grass and ferns. Here too, earlier in the year, we found frogs croaking, surrounded by a jelly like substance encasing an abundance of tiny black dots, trailing little floating legs, which were the baby tadpoles. Those tiny tadpoles would grow into frogs of all shapes and colors. They were yellow, green and sometimes black, found jumping along the sagging ditches of the meadows.

Families of rabbits lived on the drier side of the meadows. My father would frequently set traps to catch rabbits, and with great delight would bring them home, remove their skin and inside organs and prepare them so my mother could cook rabbit stew.

July 1999. The American Invasion of my home, Millstreet.

Believe it or not, my mom made the best rabbit soup that I have ever tasted and believe it or not I have never been able to find rabbit soup since. She would make it thick, as it was always filled with all kinds of vegetables from the farm, especially potatoes as she made so many meals with potatoes. Boiling them was the most popular way of cooking them with rabbits. We certainly had plenty of vegetables to eat growing up. But oh my, if I did not finish what was on my plate, then my dad would start yelling.

Only on Sunday did we have a change from an everyday diet of boiled vegetables. Then we might have boiled sausages or a big treat would be chicken, as my mom would save these chickens so she could sell their eggs and buy tea and other food items. We never went hungry, but food never changed. Breakfast everyday consisted of oatmeal. For lunch we took bread and butter, and occasionally we put jam on our sandwiches. Then we would have dinner at around 6 PM., which we called supper. During the school year we ate dinner earlier and had a light meal in the evening.

FUN WITH THE ANIMALS

The farm animals were the joy of my life, and I was very attached to them. Some of them were older than us and very much a part of our home life. Several generations were born and raised on the farm. The burial area for all the animals was up on a large field called the forth.

Padraigs Wedding—1993. Left to right: Sister Theresa, Niece Ursula Coffee, Rosemary Kelleher, Sheila and Dennis O'Sullivan, my brother.

Here the jennet (donkey) when he decided he had enough, laid down and died and was laid to rest. My dad had a large white horse which I felt he treated him more humanely that he treated a lot of his children.

I actually saw my Dad cry when his favorite horse died.

The donkey we had for many years was used by my brothers who would take him every morning to the creamery where they delivered the milk, which ultimately was churned into butter and other dairy products. The donkey was a dark brown animal that brayed and kicked like a devil. My brother only had to whistle and he came running to the gate every morning, as he knew that he was fed after he returned from the creamery. Catching the horses on the other hand was a big job as they had to be coaxed and sometimes they were uncooperative. The white mare was no problem and all one had to do was call him Paddy and he would come running. I never rode the horses but frequently rode Jennet the donkey and my legs would touch the ground as I rode, which was a big joke in my family for the 15 years that I lived in the house as my legs were so long that they touched the ground. My nickname became "Long Shanks". I loved that donkey and felt a real kinship with him. For some reason my siblings were all given names after the animals. For example Eily was the goose, Kate was the gander and Nora the fox. The animals were close to all of us. When it came to slaughter them, I just could not take it, hearing the pigs cry out for mercy as my dad was killing them. I usually took off to the fields so as not to hear their pitiful screams.

AT WORK ON THE FARM

A day in the meadow was sunshine and sweat, hard work and ambivalent feelings regarding having to work so very hard. Hayseeds and innumerable forms of insect life found their way into my hair and frequently clung to my damp back. Usually barefoot, we picked up numerous thorns and other prickly things. This annoyance was relieved by the soft feel of mossy patches beneath our feet and we developed a sixth sense about where it was safe to tread. Luckily for us there was a stream, which ran through the property and oh, the joy on a hot day to plunge into the icy water to cool down and rid ourselves of all this sticky irritation.

Back in the bog we all had to take turns digging turf which eventually, after a long period of drying became our fuel for heating and cooking. This is still done today throughout Ireland. During harvest time we had a contraption called a tumbling paddy, which was used to collect the rows of hay into big heaps. Made entirely of timber it was like a giant comb with two handles at the back. When it was full to overflowing with hay the handle was thrown forward so that the comb tumbled over and all the hay fell out. This was then used as the base for the cocks of hay, or wyndes as we called them. When the butt had been made somebody stood on it and packed the hay down while the tumbling paddy collected more hay which was packed onto the wynde until gradually it grew tall and pointed.

Standing on the wynde was a job for somebody light and agile. Pikes of hay were generally thrown up at you, and had to be pulled under your feet and danced on to firm this wavering creation. I seemed to be the guinea pig for this performance and I will admit that many a time I was scared, as somehow the hay would hide an odd scratching

August 1986. Denny and I at the Kelleher House.

briar. Now one would slide down the side of the Wynde when it had reached its peak, then it was pared of loose hay at the base and finally tied down. A piece of hay with its ends firmly embedded in the base of the wynde or as we used to call it then "A bale of hay" wound around the hay twine and knotted with it. Finally, the ball of twine was crossed over the cock and tied on the other side in the same manner.

So it continued all day, wynde after wynde was created until someone brought us the tea, which consisted of home made bread and butter and sometimes an apple cake. That was the best part of the day as we got about 15 minutes to eat and relax. It is said that hunger is a good sauce, but hunger and thirst certainly made tea in the meadows a feast with a special flavor, like

July 1999 Clara Mountain

manna from heaven. The aroma of sweet smelling hay blended with the tea. It was also a time for funny stories and riddles, which made for great laughter and fun, and the whole occasion took on the atmosphere of a gay picnic.

With tea over, we returned to work but there was a new pep in our step and gradually the wyndes rose like mini pyramids around us. Towards evening as the shadows lengthened across the fields, we gathered up our forks, rakes and other tools. And together with the horses made our weary way homewards. Eventually the hay was drawn into the barn. We all enjoyed this task, as there was an air of achievement, a fulfillment of the basic need of man to fill the barns and prepare for winter. Next to his family needs the welfare of my father's stock was closest to his heart and it was to him, like other farmer's the dread or fear to not have enough to feed his animals during the harsh days of the winter. Drawing the hay into the barn was an event all by itself. The hay was put on a horse drawn float. In the field the float was tilted up front so that the back edge lay by a wynde

July 1999. Back of Hotel Europe in Killarney.

of hay. Then the tick float ropes that were wound around an iron roller at the front of the float were unwound and tied behind the wyndes. The roller was turned, winding up the rope and bringing back the cock of hay up along the float. Once filled the horse drew home his load with the driver sitting on top of the wyndes while the children sat at the back of the float, dangling their feet while leaving the field. Drives on the float were part of our summer entertainment on the farm. The workers in the barn removed the load under the supervision of my uncle allowing the horse and float to return to the field for another load.

My uncle Patrick usually picked the hay up and one of us took it from him, and passed it back to another who packed it in the back of the barn. While the barn was being loaded we had and enjoyed our brief rest in between delivery of the next load of hay. Finally with the last load stashed away, we were grateful that this marked

Brother Dennis O'Sullivan on our farm down the Kales by a bale of hay.

the end of the haymaking season. When the barn was full of soft golden hay we knew our animals were safe against the ravages of winter no matter how harsh it might be.

The seeds we had planted in the spring grew through the summer months, and as the crops ripened the difference between them became evident as the wheat turned a golden brown and the oats, a butter yellow. Cutting the corn in

the autumn meant another chapter in the winding down of the years work and equally important this was a time when all the neighbors came to help one another. Now the biggest performance that occurred on the farm was the thrashing and the cutting of corn. The wheat would be thrashed into grain, which would eventually be turned or ground into flour for our bread and other baking needs. Seeing the threshing going on at other farms made us wonder who would be next?

1999. Cathy (Kit) Washabaugh, Julie, & Jenny her daughters.

It was like one big party as that was a time when some of the men would meet one another only once a year, at threshing time. This social event gave them a time to discuss all that had happened throughout the year. Each person had a specific job to perform. Some of them the passed the bales of wheat and threw the shaves to those on top of the thresher.

Now the main event occurred when the little trap door was opened and the golden grain poured into jute bags. These were paper bags and filled four inches or so from the top, sealed and were exchanged for empty bags. The full bags were carted across the haggard to the loft for the winter. Underneath the loft was the stall, which was the place the cows were milked and housed for the winter. On the day of thrashing, the men worked steadily, breaking only for dinner and tea. Truly, this had an air of good fellowship and fun. The haggard or barn is where the men and children stayed while the women remained in the kitchen preparing food for workers who had big appetites. It was a sad moment for us children to see the end of threshing, as we knew that this just happened once a year.

1963. Meg and Cathy right front, with family.

The geese and ducks returned to the fields and were delighted to find a feast waiting them, as some of the corn and other grain was spilled on the ground. This was party time for them and they feasted for several days during their harvest thanksgiving.

My uncle who lived with us took on the responsibility of collecting the cows from the field and bringing them in for milking. He, along with the help of my brothers and sisters milked the cows, a task I never mastered. When milking the cows my brothers and sisters sat on stools known as blocks because they were made of solid wood supported with three legs. The milkers sat down with a bucket between their knees and rested their forehead on the cow's silky body. Evening milk time was an enjoyable time, I must admit I think I was the only person in the family who never milked a cow, and that was related to the fact that left home when I was fifteen years old. At first the milk hit the bucket with a sharp metallic sound and as it filled up mellowed to a drowsy hum and the cold bucket grew warm between their legs. Milking time was singing time, or it could be just dreaming time. I have seen some cows kick their milkers and send them sprawling in the middle of the barn. The milkers carried the buckets full of milk to the churns, which we called tanks and were situated on the stands outside the stalls, and around the top of each tank was a muslin cloth through which the milk was strained. Then it was taken to the creamery and sold to be made into various dairy products.

Back of Hotel Europe. Jenny & Julie Washabaugh.

1999—Margaret Mary Becker. Down the Kales on my brothers farm at: Claraghatlea, Millstreet, County Cork Ireland. Clara Mountain in the background.

MEAT STORAGE, BIRTHING AND OTHER THINGS

I visualize all the hog meat hanging in our kitchen and near the fireplace. My father would cut and salt the meat, eventually removing the meat to cut into bacon strips then using the remaining pieces for boiled dinners. Beyond this, we really didn't store much in the way of meat as chickens and geese as well as turkeys were killed for only special occasions like Christmas and Easter. My sister Nora was great when it came to preparing for the holidays. The house was transformed over night with bright decorations and she also helped prepare the holiday meal with all the trimmings. We were all caught up with the holiday spirit.

BABY SITTING THE PIGLETS

As a child growing up in Ireland, I recall what a treat it was to stay up all night, and watch the mother pig take care of her newborn piglets. This was done in our kitchen with the floor covered with straw made into a bed. The object of our all night vigil was to prevent the mother pig from rolling on her little piglets and suffocating them. I usually worked the midnight shift with my sister Eileen and during the night she cooked the best pancakes with apples and blueberries. That is why I really enjoyed staying up and taking care of the piglets, since the rest of the family was asleep. The sow and her piglets slept in the kitchen for about a week, then they were returned to their own home out in the barn.

GOING TO SCHOOL

Going to school in the winter mornings through the gravel roads had its own beauty. The bushes and briars took on unearthly shapes of frozen rigidity, and the trees glittered with outstretched arms like graceful ballerinas. The beauty was absolutely breath taking. My dad did drive us to school in the bad weather. This was done in a horse and trap. He would get the horse and trap ready and we would all pile into the trap, with some of us sitting on the floor. He did have a big leather rug, which we all covered ourselves with and the comfort of keeping the rain out was one of the positive things he did for us. Sometimes when it was raining hard he would be waiting for us outside the school. This was a great luxury for us and we were grateful. principal regarding my sister Eileen's condition stating that she had to bathe her feet to reduce the swelling she endured from her teacher. That was unusual as I was never

1999—My school in Millstreet. Cathy & daughters, me, and my husband Jay.

allowed to say anything negative about those teachers and when I did I was simply beaten more.

On the nicer days when my father would not pick us up we managed to find the longer way home from school, through the fields, shedding our heavier clothes and shoes to romp in sheer freedom. Perhaps my father knew of this but never let on. Education was important in our home and discipline went hand and hand with it. This is all to my parents credit. While we may have complained at the time, we benefited from this priority, which was to see us grow up as well educated as we could be. Summer days came at last. We welcomed it and the freedom it brought from the shackles of winter. When the warm days were firmly established we kicked off our heavy boots and long black stockings and danced through the warm grass in delight.

The day in school was just an unwelcome interlude then between the morning trek and the return home, and if the journey to school took about thirty minutes, the coming home could take anything up to two hours. My uncle at that time worked at the side of the road breaking large stones into small ones, which in turn were used for various holes in the repair of the roads. I would frequently stop and talk with him and he would give me a penny, which I used to buy candy.

When eating there were never enough dishes to go around so we shared the dishes with one another. This time was very stressful for me as if we laughed and my dad did not approve we were verbally reprimanded. However, education was encouraged in our home as each day after school we all had to sit around a large wooden table and do our homework. Anyone caught talking too much or goofing off was punished. Discipline was the rule in my home.

My sister Mary was a nursing supervisor in a hospital in Surry, England, who developed cancer, in 1951. I went to see her, as a student nurse who was in training with me, her name was Mary Hennessy, who informed me, that I should go and see my sister, since she was very sick, and if I did not go now it may be too late. Her sister worked with my sister at another hospital. The matron of her hospital asked me why she never mentioned her family. I looked at

Mary O'Sullivan, my sister.

her and said "Neither do I" I now know that since I did not have anything positive to say, I felt things were better unsaid. That phrase "1 love you" growing up in Ireland was never mentioned and today I do not blame them for their many inadequacies. I blame them for their lack of education 60 years ago. My sister Mary had only negative memories of her childhood, just like myself, so why bother to open old wounds to complete strangers.

UNIVERSITY OF CORK

My niece Rosemary Kelleher graduated from the University of Cork in 1997

1997—**Rosemary Kelleher's graduation with father and brother.**

and is presently teaching there. In Cork city there are many areas to be explored, even the flea market! The University of Cork campus is about a 15-mile walk up Washington Street from Grand Parade. This college presently has a student body of about 10,000. Their famous library know as The Boole library, opened 1985 was named after George Boole (1815–1864) considered the father of modern computer logic. He was also the first professor of math in the College. Not too far from the College is the Cork public museum.

DIFFERENT ACCENTS

The Dubliners find Corkonians incomprehensible at times, and vice versa. But after a day or two, visitors become attuned to the Cork lilt and often find they pick up certain intonations themselves.

The cork accent takes some getting used to. The communication problem is not confined to visitors overseas either as even Millstreet lies in the Barony of Dunhallow in the northwest corner of County cork. The town nestles snugly at the foot of the Clara Mountains in the lush green valley of the River

Blackwater. Dunhallow is not too far from Millstreet and it is renowned for its natural beauty and friendly people, as well as characterized by its quaint rural area.

Cork City is the major metropolis of the south, with a population about 135,000; it is the second largest city in the Republic. Corkonians prefer to refer to it as "Ireland's Cultural Capitol". The name Cork derives from the Irish or (Gaelic) Corkage, meaning a marshy place, blaming the river Lee on which it was built because of the marsh. When the marsh was drained the river was divided into two main streams, which flow through the city, giving it a profusion of picturesque quays and bridges. That famous Irish song derived it name from the title 'On the banks of my own lovely Lee'. The population figure of Cork is also misleading since many people with families prefer to live outside the congestion of Cork City. Places such as Carrigaline and Ballincolig have eased Corks city congested traffic areas. The buses tend to be over crowded, and travel is difficult despite the use of one-way streets. The main street in Cork is Patrick street, where you will find the statue of Father Matthew who was the founder of the Pioneers Pin which requires a commitment that one takes to remain all their lives alcohol free. This movement spread to Scotland, England, and the United States.

DRISHANE

This is a big landmark in Ireland, a 15th century castle. It is where the rich, when I was growing up, sent their children to boarding school. Dating back to 1609, the school is located on 500 acres of land overlooking the town of Millstreet. My brother in California owns land across the road from Drishane. Drishane has a rich history of Irish culture. The O'Keefe's were early settlers and eventually the clan was routed by the Anglo Normans.

In the middle of the 13th century the McCarthy clan came from Kerry. From the 13th century to the 18th century this family dominated the history of Münster and particularly this area. The outstanding characteristic of the McCarthy chiefs was their love of their land. They owed no loyalty to Church or Kingdom but were loyal to their clan and held their land through thick and thin. The person who built Drishane was named Doormat who was the son of Lord Musketry. This tower has withstood all the varying fortunes of successive owners and is today a national monument. From about 1261 to 1641 the McCarthy family resided in Drishane and fought side by side with the other Irish clans in 1641.

Though the land was confiscated this was not the end of the McCarthy influence in Drishane. In 1650 Cromwell smacked the McCarthy forces and much of the house of Drishane was destroyed. After the restoration of Charles 11 in 1660 the land was leased to those who fought against the Irish. However, they were only leases and in 1702 the land was for sale, but no Catholic was allowed to bid because of the penal laws, and the Wallis family took over the land. Thus ended 500 years of McCarthy ownership. Now the Wallis family built a beautiful residence in Drishane and also built the Protestant church in Millstreet. Their power is largely forgotten now. The Wallis family went into decline, having mortgaged their land and sold out in 1900 and Drishane was not lived in again until the year 1909 when the Sisters of the Infant Jesus bought it back. These sisters made it a learning center for girls from 1911 onwards until its closure in 1992.

CLARA MOUNTAIN

My house was situated on the bottom of Clara Mountain. Many a poet has been inspired to write about "Beautiful and Majestic Clara Mountain". Rising 1,486 feet above sea level the mountain is believed to have derived its name from the flat appearance at its summit and the gradual smooth incline into the rustic valley.

BLARNEY

To acquire the "gift of the gab" is the main reason tourists want to kiss the blarney stone. Blarney castle is about five miles from the city of Cork. The castle itself dates from the mid 15th century and was built by Cormac McCarthy, later destroyed by Cromwell forces 100 years later. Queen Elizabeth 1 of England is credited for giving it that name since she said that anything that Cormac McCarthy said was not believable. When one kisses the blarney stone the view from the battlements of the square tower is most impressive. The kissing stone is set in the battlements and to kiss it you must lie on the walk within the walls, grasp a guardrail lean your head back and touch the stone with your lips. There is always an attendant there to help.

YOUGHAL

From Cork City it takes about one hour drive to Youghal. The people go there to enjoy its sandy beaches, seaside amusement facilities and its seafood restaurants. Youghal, by contrast has a larger bay and the estuary of the river Blackwater. The most famous explorer from Youghal past was an Englishman named "Sir Walter Raleigh" once the mayor of the town.

North of Cork is Forma and Mitcheltown, and then comes Mallow with its regular meetings pertaining to its racetracks and horses. Now we go on to Kinsale where some of its back roads are so quiet that they are still used for the game of bowling and when one comes across a large crowd of men cheering, the explanation is that one team has scored a point. Bantry and Glengariff are the most popular destinations in West Cork, gateways to the most dramatic mountains of the southwest. It appears to me now that I look back on things that all my cousins left in Ireland. Of course that was years ago when employment was so bad. Now the whole scenery has completely changed. The economy is flourishing and Ireland has the highest employment in Europe. This is related to the Common Market, American and European companies coming into Ireland and building various factories, hotels, and the like.

ART WITH THE VARIOUS STONES OF CORK

County Cork is fortunate in having an abundance of excellent stones for building and sculpture, red and brown stones, flagstone states and a limestone comparable in quality to most of the most famous continental stones. The limestone is mostly pale gray with some much darker, streaked with bands of red and pink, quite widely used for ornamental work. The county thus possesses a considerable heritage of fine buildings in local stone while almost every county graveyard bears witness to the skills of local sculptors working in locally obtained material.

Prehistoric "Rock Art" circles, cup marks and the like are found on rock faces and bolder in various parts of the county and belong to the same tradition and period as the better known example of New Grange. In Downhill the northwestern part of County Cork, however exploration of local sculpture begins with the highly sophisticated Early Christian works at Tully lease. Saint Bechar known locally as Saint Ben was one of a number of saintly Englishmen who migrated to Ireland and founded monasteries here. Celtic crosses and patterns only come much later with the intensification of the struggle for Irish Independence.

CHAPTER II

OFF TO MERRY ENGLAND

The opportunity developed when a neighbor who was a nun was home for her father's funeral. I was under 15 years at the time (1943). It was my chance to return to England with her and I took full advantage of that. I joined her cloistered order, which was an experience I will never forget. It was a delight to be able to sleep alone in a bed and to look forward to three meals a day all with great variety. On the down side, in this cloistered order we were only allowed to speak for 15 minutes per day. I lasted nine months in that order. I took flight from this order in 1943. To my late and wonderful sister Eileen, who was working in a factory in England. She lived in a hostel and took me in, lined up jobs for me as a maid. I worked for Captain and Mrs. Hawks, who were nice to me and after about ten months they gave me a vacation.

My graduation. Note the pin. 1952

I returned to Ireland, and while there received a letter from them saying my services were no longer needed. My parents knew this, however, my mother sent me back to England saying, "You will get some kind of a job". I immediately went to the employment office where they were amazed that I did not even have a place to stay that night. The agency obtained a job for me in a rectory where I helped the housekeeper. It was the priest here who was instrumental in getting me into a nursery training school for a two-year course and I became certified as a nursery nurse in 1946. I completed two years training as a nursery nurse or nanny in a residential catholic orphanage in Birmingham, England. In this training they provided us with room and board and gave us a small amount of money such as about $10 per month. The nurse's uniform was pink with a white hat. This school consisted of about 20 student nurses and maybe 60 babies all under 12 months old. Here we learned how to take care of children in all areas such as nutritional, physical, and emotional. I then received a certificate stating that I was qualified as a nursery nurse or nanny. Later on I was eventually employed as a governess to a family that was more than kind to me. The family lived in a large house in a suburb of London and in addition to me had servants and a cook. Her husband was much older than her. They had two children, a baby and a toddler. She was a lovely blond lady and was just great to me. I worked there for 18 months and saved my money.

Later with money saved, I entered nurses training and upon graduation received six letters after my name, S.R.N. and S.C.M. These letters stood for State Registered Nurse and State Certified Midwife. My training took place from 1948 to 1952 at Queen Mary's Hospital for the east end of London England. I stayed there for four years as a student nurse and this included six months training in the midwifery unit. I trained in one of the poorest hospitals in the east side end of London receiving the best training that one could ever get. As a student nurse we had to sign in and out when we left the nurses home. When we worked nights about six to eight of us would take the underground train and frequently go up to the west end of London to a tea dance. This is where we would meet all kinds of people as I recall meeting this particular medical student from Istanbul, Turkey.

I remember when I was a student nurse working in the outpatient floor of Queen Mary's hospital when this lovely lady came in with some problems. She was wearing a lovely gold ankle bracelet, which was my first time seeing something like this She kept repeating, "I am a professional". I did not know what she meant so I questioned further and she informed me that she takes care of business people in the big hotels in the west end of London. The message sank in. My training school was mainly Irish, English nurses, and we did have two lovely ladies from Africa who were very delightful. In training we worked from 9am until 9 pm. with three hours off in the afternoon. We did a great deal of domestic work especially in the operating rooms where after each operation we had to wash down the room completely including the walls, operating table, and chairs. When we first started nurses training they sent us away for three months to a nursing school where we learned the basics of the medical field. My first day in the hospital before going to that school, I was sent to the operating room to hold a ladies leg as it was amputated. I knew then that I would make it as a nurse because it did not affect me in any way.

My training days were memorable, as we either worked days or nights. I will always remember night duty and how we finished at 7 am. Then three or four of us would go to the lake in the nice weather. I became good friends with a nurse by the name of Nancy Smith who married when she was in training. She often had me stay at her house since her husband was in the navy. Way back then we were not allowed to get married while in training. However, things did change and finally it was OK to get married as a student nurse. I spent many a weekend at her house, and she was a great cook, I used to take three buses to her home, as the public transportation in London was very good. In London I saw many stage plays at the west end of town. I saw Ingrid Berman and her entourage outside and I recall that her ladies in waiting were heavily made up. She was not with Rosalini then. Queen Mary's hospital had an arrangement with all the big play houses to allow the student nurses in free of charge. All we had to do was show them our identification, which stated that we were student nurses at Queen Mary's Hospital. The same applied to all the famous concert halls. We were very fortunate with all the perks we received by being student nurses.

I met this teacher of piano when I was in nurses training. I was taking care of her father who had lung cancer. Since I always wanted to learn the piano I made arrangements with this lady that I would give her dad a bath once a week in her home, and for this service I would like her to teach me the piano. I did this for about one year. I finally bought a piano from a Red Cross nurse and moved it into the nurses home. Now I had my own piano to practice on, so when I completed my training I left the piano in the nurse's residence. During my break every day I would practice and I will never forget this nursing super visor saying to me one day "Sheila, was that you playing the piano"?

Was I proud of myself as then I realized how good I was progressing. Today, years later, I love to play the piano, and now I do play all my classics like "Chopin Nocturne Opus 9 No 2, and Beethoven's Sonatina in G". I loved those piano pieces and to this day I enjoy playing them. However, when I make a mistake and my husband is within hearing distance I can hear him out loud saying "Wrong note".

I then went to train as a midwife at Pembroke Hospital in Pembroke Kent, England. When there I also trained on the district under the supervision of a qualified midwife. That was great experience for me since I delivered babies in a converted train and used boxes as a crib, sometimes drawers if available. However, all I was interested in was that mother and baby survived the ordeal of being born in a train. I was rather scared at times and thank God that there was an experienced midwife with me.

We wore a navy blue outfit when working in the district, which consisted of a navy blue dress with a white roman collar like a priest. I felt very proud of this uniform and the community at large had great respect for us as nurses and midwives. I remember delivering twins on Easter morning, and the father was surprised when I informed him that his wife had twins. Apparently I said to him "The second one was not mine". That made the headline of the papers which read," Nurse said I know the second baby is not mine".

Cathy ran in Detroit's 2000 Marathon. Note cement pipe background is from Northern Concrete Pipe in Bay City, Washabaugh Family Business.

CHAPTER III

OFF TO AMERICA

Because of high unemployment Ireland for years lost it's young people who traveled to the United States and elsewhere seeking decent jobs. Well educated as we were, the future at home was at best bleak. I responded to an advertisement in a medical publication put out by Grace hospital in Detroit, offering to sponsor nurses to come to America as the hospital was understaffed. I was sponsored here by Grace hospital in January of 1955. The hospital was located on East Alexandrine street in Detroit. I worked there as a graduate nurse until I sat the state board exam. Once I passed the exam I was then capable of working as a registered nurse. I lived in the nurses home of Grace hospital, had my own bedroom, and use of all utilities which included a shared kitchen. When I came here, I was working in the delivery room, but after one month of simply passing instruments to the various doctors I became very bored, because at that time nurses were not allowed to deliver babies. However nowadays there are certified midwives here who are working as part of hospitals and their area is now known as "The Birthing Center' where only nurse midwives work there and the patients receive prenatal care and post natal care from the nurse midwives and should emergency occur they are next door to a hospital. In general these areas are now more accepted by the doctors and they work in harmony with the nurse midwife.

The training of nurses in this country is far different than in England, however the bottom line is that in both countries we all have the same goals, and that is to help the patient feel more comfortable and return home and participate in their normal daily activities. When I say the training here is far different than in England, by that I mean that in England we are taught from day one that bed side care is the most important area of nursing so we did a great deal of bed side care. However here I feel that nurses in training receive a great culture shock when they are placed in an unit and given three to four patients as a student and then when they graduate they are given double those patients and that is when culture shock becomes obvious. There are advantages and disadvantage to both types of training as over here the students are now required to go to college and receive a Bachelor in Nursing Degree could be a three or four year course. Arriving in Detroit in 1955 I learned that there were a number of nurses who came to Grace hospital via Canada who were originally from Ireland. We became fast friends and shared the culture shock of nursing in the U.S. as compared to our training back home. We were more "hands on" in England and Ireland. American nurses were more into charting and were more inclined to leave "bedside care, i.e. bathing, feeding etc to Licensed Practical Nurses and Nurses Aides. Grace hospital was located in an old and generally decaying area of the city. The nurse's residence was elegant and warm. We all had individual rooms and a shared kitchen. The living room was nicely decorated, with a large grand piano, which I played at intervals. Our kind housemother, Mrs. Dodd, was very motherly and she made sure we all signed in and out of the residence. Going to and from the hospital was easy as there was a tunnel running between the two buildings. This was especially attractive in the cold weather of Michigan or when working late shifts. Making friends in

America was easy as the Americans are by nature unassuming, much like the Irish back home. My two closest friends in America were to become bride's maids of mine later on. They were Millie Cooley and Dolores Koski. Millie was very religious and went on to do missionary work and brought her nursing skills to India and Pakistan. Dolores eventually married and is happily situated in the Upper

Dingle, Ireland, August 1986. Meg & son-in-law Tom filleting Pollock.

Peninsula of Michigan. I have lost contact with Millie but remain in contact with Dolores. One of my favorite dinning out places was a Chinese restaurant near the hospital. It was a popular place for all the nurses in residence as the food was good, prices reasonable and we could run a tab until we were paid. My favorite food was egg foo young and I still like to order it to this day.

My first St. Patrick's day celebration turned out to be a real experience. Americans celebrate the day as a special event and back home it was more or less another day. Eight of us went out to dinner. We left the restaurant when my girlfriend Joan realized she left her purse in the restaurant. She sent her boy friend back to retrieve it and somehow some people thought he was stealing it.

July 1997, Voyageur Restaurant, St. Clair MI. Nephew Tom Villalobos & wife Ngoc, from Vietnam.

So, what happened next? A fight broke out!

What could be more Irish? The police were called in and we were all lined up against the wall. I was so scared as I had never seen anything like that. Eventually, we were notified of a court date and we could only think of the hospital firing us. Appearing in court as the combatants, Joan's boy friend and someone else were charged with disorderly conduct and fined. Much to our relief that was the end of the episode and nothing was reported to the hospital.

CULTURE SHOCK

Coming from a small town in Ireland to London and eventually Detroit, one realizes the pay offs between small towns and large metropolitan areas. There is not the same closeness one has in a small community versus the large city but there is much more to do in the city. The nurses often received passes or discount tickets to many cultural events. I remember seeing the Detroit Symphony Orchestra in a performance conducted by Paul Paray. We were close by to the Detroit Institute of Arts, downtown theaters and department stores. From downtown Detroit we could look across at Windsor, Canada. Going east on Jefferson perhaps two miles away was Belle Isle, a beautiful island park in the Detroit River. We spent much time there enjoying the beach, swimming, boating and picnicing. There was an amusement park called Bob-Lo, which was reachable, only by excursion boats. Just to take the boat ride was a thrill by itself.

Today, the major down town department stores have disappeared to the suburbs, the Bob-Lo excursion is no longer in existence and as one might expect, some good things and bad things have happened. When I arrived in the city of Detroit the population was two million and now it has slipped to just under one million, the result of urban flight. On the other hand, Grace hospital to day is part of a major medical center, and is still affiliated with Wayne State University. The Detroit Symphony now performs in the historic

Orchestra Hall with its perfect acoustics. Major sports stadiums are now in the downtown area as well as a new opera house and numerous theaters. Belle Isle is still a gem and the location for a major Grand Prix racing event. The Gold Cup boat race is held annually on the Detroit River and the city is showing signs of recovery throughout.

THE GERMAN CONNECTION

Cherry Pink and Apple Blossom Pink, recorded by Perez Prado and his Orchestra will forever remind me of my dear friend, Doctor Walter Uher. This song is played with a trumpet which Walter dubbed "The constipated trumpet". Every time I hear this song I think of Walter and the good times we had together

Walter was here from Germany for advanced training and once we met, we went out frequently, enjoying each other's company and I actually thought that we would develop a serious relationship, only to find that this was not to be. I learned that Walter had returned to Germany to marry a woman whose both families, his and hers had pre-arranged for him to marry. It was devastating news for me to find out about this arrangement. Somehow we all have the strength to overcome our disappointments and over the years we maintained a contact and friendship, which has lasted to this day, writing and calling at least annually. Walter is now divorced and remarried. He is not in good health and is dying according to his second wife. It seems the constipated trumpet will not play soon.

Ring of Kerry in Killarney. Daughter Cathy with her children Julie & Jenny.

A SIMPLE START TO A LONG LIFE TOGETHER

I was a nurse in a critical care unit of Old Grace Hospital, which we referred to as "Death Valley" and became friends with the daughter of one of my patients. She arranged a double date through my husband-to-be, Julius Adrian

Becker or Jay, as he is better known. Jay lined up his best friend Jack as my escort and the four of us went to a German Sing-A-Along place called The Dakota Inn. We could only stay there for a short period of time, as I had to be on duty early the following morning.

Going to Handel's Messiah Concert with husband Jay.

The following Saturday Jay and I met quite by accident at the Chapel of the Little Flower which is within walking distance of old Grace and across the street from where he was working as a divisional credit manager. We both had gone in there for confession. We met and chatted at the back of the Church and I mentioned that I was going out to San Francisco, California with my girl friend, also a nurse to visit my sister Eileen and brother Pat. He gave me his address and asked me to send him a post card, which I did. Upon my return, Jay called for a date and I accepted. Meanwhile, Jack knew of this and asked me out for a date at the same time. I hemmed and hawed and didn't have the heart to tell him about my arrangement with Jay but managed to fumble some sort of excuse, which he reluctantly accepted. Jack was best man at our wedding, May 4, 1957, which culminated a whirlwind courtship, which began in early October of 1956. The engagement ring came at Christmas time along with a fur jacket. I still have the fur coat today believe it or not! P.S., the ring too.

GETTING STARTED WITH HOUSE HUNTING

It didn't take long for us to find a house that was to be our home for 24 years. Located on busy Telegraph Road, a divided road more like a boulevard with its grassy islands, the house was acquired through assumption of the first and second mortgages in late January of 1957. We managed to pool together

$3,000 and with an additional $3,000 loaned to us by my husband's brother Francis and his wife Peggy, we assumed the mortgage of approximately $8,600. The sad news is that the owners got hardly anything out of the sale as the second mortgage represented money borrowed for a failing business. We later learned that the husband developed cancer and died soon after.

GETTING MARRIED FROM NURSES HOME

I used the nurse's home as my own home, therefore I decided that I would like to get married from there. The photographer took pictures around the lovely black piano in the living room. My bridesmaids were the two nurses I met the day I arrived in this Country.

We had no other financial help in paying wedding expenses as my family back in Ireland could not help and my husband's parents were deceased. With limited resources we had a wonderful wedding at Blessed Sacrament Cathedral, which is the parish Jay was raised in, and his father was organist there for 12 years. My husband's background as well as his family will be detailed later on. I will only say it was totally different than mine in Ireland. The something borrowed was my wedding gown from one of my close Irish

In the front of our house in Birmingham. Brother in Law Jack McSweeney and my sister Joan.

nurse friends. Midway through the mass, Jay's knees buckled and he left the altar briefly with Jack, the best man. This created a stir in the congregation as one of our non-Catholic friends whispered, "Has he changed his mind"? All went well, however, as we headed out for luncheon at The Park Sheldon hotel for the immediate family and participants. The evening reception was held in the finished basement of our new home with food catered from a Mr. Curry, a restaurant owner and friend of my husband who provided typical Irish food. The man who gave me away was from Millstreet who settled in New York City.

I guess that the Irish are famous for having its share of tenors and Joe was no exception as he provided vocal entertainment for us all.

HONEYMOON TIME AND FALSE LEADS

It seems everyone wants to know where you plan to go on your honeymoon and to be honest, we just planned to travel somewhere where there was water and sandy beaches. We strategically placed brochures and maps around the house for all sorts of exotic places to throw off the curious. We spent our first night in a motel about two miles from our home called "Easy Rest" a name some people would consider a misnomer for honeymooners. The next day it was mass at St Agatha's church and then off to the water and beaches.

Driving along the southern shore of Lake Erie we stayed at a lovely place in Conneaut. Ohio, just a few miles west of the Pennsylvania border. After a few days there, what next? On our loosely planned honeymoon we decided to head

west to Alton, Illinois, Jay's hometown and where his sister Catherine, her husband Henry and their daughter Susan Kay lived. For whatever reason they could not make it up for our wedding. We hit it off right away and for me it was a lasting friendship. Over the years we traveled by train or car to spend Thanksgiving Day with them, which turned into

Boardwalk, Clearwater Beach

an annual event. One memorable Thanksgiving dinner, we arrived to ham instead of turkey as the big bird was put in the oven on broil, not bake. The turkey was excellent on the following day.

Now I will go into some length pertaining to my husband's background, which was, to say the least, completely opposite to mine. His parents were Rene Louis and Angela Becker (nee Landzettel) and both were deeply involved in the arts, especially music. Recent articles about his father appeared in the AMERICAN ORGANIST, a century old publication of the American Guild of Organist and was later picked up and translated in the Dutch publication called de Orgelvriend. I will quote with attribution to the author, Gene Scott and the publisher's excerpts from the article.

"The musical tradition goes back well into the 19th century to the French province of Alsace where my husbands great grandfather, Jean Baptiste Becker grew up. The tradition includes a connection with Johannes Brahms and Jay's father Rene.

Jean Baptiste Becker lived on a farm, but cultivated a love of music and became an accomplished musician and teacher. He passed this on to his six children. All were trained from an early age in piano, violin, organ, and voice. His son Edouard excelled and became the organist at the Cathedral of Chartres and later the Strasbourg Cathedral. This was in the 1860s and 1870s.

Edouard and his wife Adele raised a daughter Lucie and five sons, Edouard, Lucien, Camille, Julian and Rene in the town of Bischeim, in Alsace. Rene was born in 1882. He along with all entered the Conservatory of Strasbourg. Some noted musicians at the time were Rene's teachers. They included Ernest Munch, whose son Charles became music director and conductor of The Boston Symphony Orchestra. Another was Fritz Blumer, a pupil of Franz Liszt. Rene studied advanced composi- **gift.** tion under Carl Somborn, a pupil

Dec. 1999—New Office Chair, a Christmas gift.

of Joseph Rheinberger. His organ instruction came from Adolphe Gessner, a Swiss organist.

The connection with Johannes Brahms? Once a year Brahms came to the Strasbourg Conservatory to perform a piano recital. In the mid 1890s young Rene was chosen to turn pages for the maestro during his recital. It was the supreme honor especially for a conservatory student.

In 1904, Rene came to the United States and joined two of his brothers, Lucian and Camille, in St. Louis and formed The Becker Conservatory of Music. Upon the death of Camille and Lucian's desire to move westward to Portland, Oregon, the history of the Conservatory came to an end. Over the next 40 years, Rene's compositions, 425 with well over 100 published, were performed by artists of the day. His works were published by all the major publishers.

It was in 1910 when he married Angela Landzettel. Devoted to the fine arts, she was an accomplished musician in her own right, and was known as a painter and poet. Several of her piano and organ compositions were published. The music that issued from the piano and pens of Rene and Angela Becker in those productive years of their marriage seemed unrelenting.

The couple moved to Belleville, Illinois in 1912, the year after their first child Catherine was born. Then came Rene Claude in 1913 and Francis Joseph in 1915, by which time they had moved to Alton, Illinois, where they lived for the next 15 years. While there, Rene continued to teach, perform in concert, and was the organist at the St. Peter and Paul Cathedral in Alton. Last but not least in the family came Julius (or Jay) who was born in 1929.

In 1930, Rene became the first organist at the newly built Blessed Sacrament Cathedral in Detroit. A member of the American Guild of Organists, he along with my husband's brother Francis founded the Palestrina Institute to teach area organists Gregorian chant and liturgical music. He played at the installation of Cardinal Mooney and Bishop Woznicki. After 1943, he moved to St. Alphonsus Church in Dearborn and was organist there until he retired in 1952 at the age of 70. Rene L. Becker died in 1956 after a long illness, leaving behind a legacy of music for his family, the Church, and the ages.

As before, the Becker family legacy was family policy. From their early years, all of Rene and Angela's children had to learn a musical instrument. Although Rene Claude eventually went into banking, music was more of a serious affair for Francis as he became organist at St. Mary's Church in suburban Royal Oak, and in the 1950's was the organist and choir director at St. Benedict Church in Highland Park.

Daughter Catherine moved back to Alton, Illinois, to marry her childhood sweetheart and to teach piano and voice. My husband continued with piano and organ and has had many music students. After returning from the air force in 1954, he abandoned a career in music and entered into banking `becoming a vice president, while retaining his love of music as his avocation. This love of music continued, as he became organist and music director at our parish, St. Eugene in Detroit, on a pro bono basis. Meanwhile Jay preserves the family's musical tradition, while his daughter Cathy and her daughters Julie and Jenny are active in piano studies. Everywhere in our home there is music, including many yellow scores, published and unpublished, rich reminders of the life style and work of Rene and Angela Becker. I deeply regret that Jay's parents were both deceased when I came over from Ireland.

My husband grew up in Blessed Sacrament parish and perhaps if you can attribute this to politics, (after all his father was the organist and choir director of the church); he became the youngest acolyte in the parish history. He continued his education in the parochial system and upon graduation continued his education in music under his father's tutelage. In 1950, barely missing military service in World War 2, he was at the perfect age for the Korean war and rather than being drafted, chose to enlist in the Air Force, spending 30 months in Japan in his four year enlistment, functioning as a radio operator. Upon his discharge as a Staff Sergeant in1954, he used his G.I. bill to obtain a degree in accounting rather than return to a musical career. While he was in Japan he organized a choir at Johnson Air Base near Tokyo. One of his fondest memories was bringing the base choir to Tokyo to a Church called St. Anthony and appropriately the choir sang his fathers mass in honor of St. Anthony. Also, along with members of the choir and the Air Force chaplain, climbed Mt. Fuji in 1953 to perform at the top, the first Catholic High Mass on Mt. Fuji. The mass performed was in Gregorian chant. The Air Force chaplain and my husband still correspond and share their memories. In our living room standing in a corner is a six-foot wooden staff or pole he used in climbing Mt. Fuji. According to Jay, you purchased the staff at the base of the mountain for a nominal amount of money and as you ascended the mountain there were 10 major stations for resting plus numerous sub stations along the was where your staff was branded with a branding iron for the incredible amount at that time of 10 yen or about three cents per brand. Reaching the top of Mt. Fuji was the ultimate goal and the reward was to have three pennants, one being the Japanese flag as well as a string of bells attached to the staff. Going down the mountain the bells would ring out the news that you had made it to the top which gave encouragement to those still climbing to keep going After nearly fifty years the pennants have faded but the staff, with all it's brands remains like a solid rock. And a reminder of a memorable adventure my husband had climbing the sacred mountain of Japan, called Mt. Fuji.

CHAPTER IV

THE EARLY YEARS

Our neighborhood was about as far out as you could be and still be in the City of Detroit. Since city employees were required to live in the city we had an abundance of police, firemen and other city personnel in our area. Our neighbor to the south of us was a homicide detective and to the north of us was a policeman. It was a friendly neighborhood filled with young people struggling to raise families and pay off mortgages. My husband continued to attend night school with his major in accounting and also changed jobs to work for a local bank, which was to be his employer for the next 31 years.

Our first daughter, Margaret was born in June 1958. She was named for no one in particular except the Margaret part was tied into my sister-in-law Peg. Meg came to us past her due date, as I was unable to have a normal delivery and went through a caesarian section at the Old Grace Hospital. My husband was on the road for the bank at this time and when he called in to the hospital was told the baby was due any minute. He was so excited he spilled coffee from his thermos all over his shirt, racing down to the hospital. Like all good dad's he was there when I needed him. At this time our parish, St. Eugene was holding a fun fair and Jay bought a string of tickets and wouldn't you know he won and selected as his prize, a basket full of baby food.

I have always had a penchant for fresh air; summer or winter. We had a screened in addition to our house in the back, and in the middle of winter I would bundle up our little Meg, place her under warm coverings in a pram and put her out in the room addition for an hour or two, much to the shock and surprise of our neighbors. This caught on in the neighborhood eventually and to this day I believe strongly in allowing our children to develop both indoors and outdoors. Just look at their rosy cheeks when they come in from the winter air!

My husband announced one day at work that our second child was on the way and, in matter of fact, would be born March 22, 1960. A girl named Barbara felt this was too much for him to come out with the exact date and challenged him by betting a dollar that he was wrong. This turned out to be the easiest dollar we ever made as we were told that I was scheduled for a Caesarian section on that date. When the facts came out he offered to rescind the bet, but Barbara was stubborn and lost graciously. Our second child Catherine Angela arrived on schedule. Both names have some family tradition, unlike our daughter Meg.

My husband's grandmother was Catherine Landzettel and his sister was Catherine Angela. His mother was Angela so it was automatic that we chose these names. During my stay at Grace Hospital our Meg somehow got under the sink and we thought, at least at that time, possibly swallowed some furniture scratch remover. My husband ran her over to the closest hospital, which was in our Redford area, and her stomach was pumped out. She was deemed to be OK but Jay insisted she stay at the hospital for observation. So it became double duty for my Jay as he would routinely visit Meg at the Redford hospital and then journey down to old Grace hospital to visit me, and our new born" Kit", as we nick named her.

PARTY TIME ANYONE?

Early on I guess we developed a reputation for getting people together, within or outside of our neighborhood to party. Any excuse was acceptable even to toast the Queen of England. And, do you

Jay Becker & his lovely niece Pamela Wilde, daughter of Rene' and Helen Becker.

know, we have had many good friends and neighbors over the years. For example Barb and Dan O'Rourke who lived about three doors from us would host an Easter egg hunt and our immediate neighbors would open up their swimming pool for all the kids to use. Parish friends had similar events, which included Christmas Eve for an open house at the Duquettes. We carried on this tradition when we moved to Birmingham.

OUR PARISH ST. EUGENE

Our involvement in St. Eugene parish became almost an addiction. It was a young parish founded in 1954 by Fr. Louis F. Fournier who chose the name to

honor his father. Our parish was one of five named for St. Eugene in the entire country. St. Eugene I was a Pope and Martyr, consecrated Pope on August 10, 657 AD. He was Roman and the son of Rufinius, who belonged to the first or Aventine Quarter of the City. This was the first of the seven ecclesiastical regions into which Rome had been divided by the Popes from the earliest times.

His reign was short but he maintained the integrity of the Church during a period of upheaval in the City of Rome. He was buried at St. Peter's on June

2000: Julie Washabaugh, Meg Becker, Jenny Washabaugh at Jay Becker's Concert: Voices of Light. Passing out programs.

2, 659 A.D. The previous was gleaned from a 25th anniversary book in 1969 celebrating St Eugene parish.

The revenue from ads and other donations paid the cost of our new Allen Organ, which replaced a very tired out Wurlitzer. Our new organ cost a resounding $15,000 installed.

Father Fournier or "Father Louie" as he was fondly called was a shy man who was raised in the town of Hancock in Michigan's Upper Peninsula. He hated to talk about money but really had little choice. After all, we had to pay off the debt for construction of our church, which was housed in a "U shape" building. On one side of the U was the grade school, the church on the other side of the "U", which was expected to eventually become the gymnasium. The back of the two sides were connected with a parish hall and additional classroom space.

The sisters of Notre Dame de Namur in Cincinnati, Ohio agreed to provide a number of nuns to partially help us in staffing the school. Of course this meant we had to build a convent and, add more debt to service. At one point our parish debt exceeded $300,000, which was a lot of money back in the 50's and 60's.

The parish was a beehive of activity. We had all the usual parish organizations going such as Boy Scouts, Girl Scouts, Ushers Club, Altar Society, Men's Club, Choir, and "Good Old Days". A one-day event held in Edgewater Park after Labor Day, which netted $20,000 annually. More later about the "Good Old Days".

I was involved in the Girls Scouts and Altar Society, making sure our two daughters became active members of our troop. Scouting was totally new to me and I learned a lot from this experience. Our girls earned many badges and made me very proud.

Meanwhile, my husband directed the choir and played the organ at Sunday masses, pro bono, until the parish was financially able to pay a full time organist, but he continued to direct the choir.

Jay was active in the Men's Club and became its president in 1969. It sponsored various activities for the children of the parish, movies and bingo for the children, Halloween parties and physical activities such as baseball and basketball. The physical activities were geared for the boys but a year before he became president he convinced the board to sponsor a girls league. The team took on names of gems like the Rubies, Sapphires, Diamonds, Pearls, Emeralds and the like. The league was an instant success and drew more fans than the boy's league did. In August we held a playoff on a Saturday, an all day event of baseball and summer time food. The organization was self supporting through membership dues, fund raising drives like paper drives, sales of fruit cakes and crocks of cheese during the holiday season. The monthly meetings always turned out to be a night out for the boys as tables were set up later for nickel dime poker, euchre, and pinochle.

GOOD OLD DAYS

A major source of funds to pay off the parish debt turned out to be the one day use of Edgewater Park for an event called The Good Old Days, a theme based on the 1890's dress and tradition. The amusement park operated during the summer and closed right after Labor Day. The Wagner family, owner of the park, generously offered the parish the use of the Park for a Sunday following the closing of Edgewater for the season. The first event took place in 1966, and like the man who ate the first raw oyster, not knowing what to expect we all dove in with various committees to organize raffle tickets, and attractions besides the rides. Our parish prize for years was a brand new Mustang, which in those days cost us $2000, which today would hardly be a good down payment. The first year event was highly successful and became a precursor of future Good Old Days events.

Oct. 2001. Granddaughter Jenny playing baseball on our farm.

From then on we were completely involved and my husband became what was to be, ticket chairman with one exception when he became general chairman in 1970. We brought something new to the good old days fundraiser and that was the farmers market. Produce from our ten-acre farm in South Lyon. The produce was sold at give away prices and added to the bottom line to the proceeds turned over to the parish. The year Jay was general chairman, at a get together at the parish hall afterwards, Father Fournier said he did not expect this much from the "Parish Tinkler", referring of course to his organ/choir directing. Jay then said he felt like a "June Bride", sore but satisfied. We took in over $21,000 that year and made it tough for the next chairman.

THE FARM

We purchased a ten-acre farm in Salem Township near South Lyon in late 1969. I have always wanted to have a piece of acreage and we took off for the city of Farmington to look up someone who had been a close friend of Jay and was now the President of a bank in Farmington. We had hoped that he would be able to guide us to some acreage and sat in the lobby of the bank until we could wait no longer. We then walked along the main street and found a real estate agency, Gringle Reality. We stated what we wanted and she said she thought she had the perfect piece of property for us, out Eight mile road in Salem Township. When we saw it I said to Jay, "This is a bit of Ireland" and I wanted it now!

1999. Our first pumpkin picking party on our farm with friends from St. Eugene Parish.

The price was $20,000 and we made a deposit on it. Meanwhile, the owner of the property a retired teacher, living in Florida, called some of his old neighbors who said he was a fool to sell the 10 acres at that price and of course, we were then advised that he wanted $25.000. We backed off. Then a few weeks later, I said that maybe we should make a counter offer and we reluctantly did, increasing our offer to $22,000. He then countered with a price of $24,500 and I had a heck of a time getting my husband to agree to it but eventually he did, selling off some investments to raise cash of $7500 and placing the balance on land contract.

Little did we know what joy and friendship this would bring to us and our many friends at St. Eugene and elsewhere. Right away we searched for equipment to carry on our "gentleman farming" and were highly successful, finding a 1940's John Deere tractor, plow, disk and other items. Thanks to our good friends the Duquettes, Draftas, Rutkowskis (who were raised in a farm near Ubly, Michigan who we referred to as the Ubly American), Martins, Scotts, on and on. This unlikely group dove in feet first, planting fruit and nut trees, plowing the land, researching seed catalogs for the latest variety of seeds and it just all took off. It was nothing to see 12 to 15 cars parked on our land, as the farm was the place to go and bring the kids. We labored all day and partied afterwards, building a large fire and bringing in bushels of corn, fresh picked for cooking, tomatoes and the other fruits of our labor. We grew, harvested and shared all the things we raised on our farm and during "The Good old Days" event bushels of produce were brought in for the farmers market. All the kids had a ball and would pick a watermelon or cantaloupe and bring it back across the stream or rivulet by our famous two seater out house and feast away. This two seater caused some initial problems with our neighbors to the east of us. Needing a place "to go" was an immediate problem and our friends, the Baczynskis designed and built a magnificent structure, which we set in the back of the farm.

The neighbors to our east objected to this magnificent structure and called the health department in Washtenaw County to report us. This two seater was located in the extreme back of our farm, hidden by a grove of trees. We were cited and met with the inspector who was immediately impressed with the structure, making a couple of suggestions to improve it (screening to keep the

Cross at St. Eugene's Church, made from wood at Becker's Acres Barn. 1976

Cross #2 made from the center beam at the Salem Township Barn (1911) at Holy Name Church in Birmingham, MI. 2002.

bugs out) and approved the structure but said it should technically be 500 feet away from a body of water, and it was located by this tiny stream. He said he would approve this structure and suggest to the complainant that it should be moved to the fence across from his home to remove this violation. Having the choice of keeping it where it was or next to his house the complainant backed off. This was a victory, which the inspector shared in. At the front of the property was an old barn, built in1911 with an attached silo. Across from this was a pond, which would freeze over in the winter. Ice skating became another use for our land and afterwards we had cookouts, bringing from home boiled dinners and lots of hot drinks. The barn eventually came down as the result of my husband backing the tractor in and knocking down one of the main beams. The pond in later years dried up which ended our winter fest. The barn wood though, was to have new life. Our friend Bob Duquette fashioned a cross out of one of the beams and brought it to St. Eugene's for the Lenten Season. We were unaware of this and when we attended Sunday Mass we saw this beautiful cross

on the altar and the priest said this wood now had new life, coming down from a barn, which had collapsed. Then it dawned on us! It was wood from our old barn and contributed to years of service, even to this day as a Lenten symbol. The Detroit News, Palm Sunday edition, carried a story and picture of the cross. Following the closing of our old parish with its 35-year history, the cross was taken to a neighboring parish, St. Gerard where the tradition of putting up the cross during the Lenten season continues.

When we bought the land we acquired an abstract, which we turned in for title insurance. The abstract revealed a history going back to the early 1800's. Eight mile road separated Oakland County from Washtenaw County, which created a problem when we acquired the ten acres in Washtenaw County.

July 1999. Killarney Muckross Castle. Jenny and Julie Washabaugh.

Mrs. Buffington, who lived and died in the farmhouse in Oakland County across from our farm, had her death recorded in Oakland County. But, she also owned the ten acres of land across the street from her home in Washtenaw County. This resulted in a mild panic attack for the closing as her death was recorded in Oakland County but not in Washtenaw County. Thanks to Mrs. Gringle, this mess was quickly resolved when the records were straightened out with her death duly recorded in Washtenaw County records and then we were able to close our purchase of the land.

This brought so many families and us together and literally we raised our families on the farm. I remember how my husband and Tony Martin spent a week of vacation time to plant 2000 pine and spruce trees ordered from the State of Michigan in a period of over 90 degrees temperatures in the month of May. The temps set all kinds of "high" records. I remember too the time we left our family dog "Deputy Dog" on the farm and when half way home the question was asked, "Where 's Dep? We quickly turned back to see Deputy sitting on top of a knoll, waiting patiently for our return looking out from his spot. There was almost always a stop at Guernsey Dairy in Northville for ice cream and during the fourth of July celebration we made sure we stopped on the hill overlooking the fire works in Northville to say our oohs and aahs. Seems like the fireworks got better every year.

Our daughters and their friends had as much fun on the farm as we did. We had a number of camp outs sitting around warm and peaceful fires. Tents were set up for "all-nighters" and it was then I learned that my Jay was not an outdoorsman. He tried to sleep in one of the tents but could not, venturing back home but returning early in the morning with eggs, bacon, sausages, which he cooked over a smoldering, fire from the night before.

The girls asked if we could go along with them on having a pig roast out on the farm. With some reluctance we went along with this, as they would be unchaperoned throughout overnight as the piglet roasted all night over hot coals. We learned with much delight that our girls and their friends were responsible kids and don't we all worry about things like this, loosening up on the strings just enough to let them take on doing the right thing? By the way we returned to the farm the following afternoon to find plenty of left overs from the pig roast. The kid's were good cooks and surprised us.

We could not strike water but we did strike oil. First, the water. Ed Riehl, a member of St. Eugene's brought out his divining rod to our farm and we poked around with it until it seemed to tremble enough for Ed to say, "This is the spot". Bob Duquette brought out a well pounder, pipe was bought and away we went, pounding the pipe into the ground, followed by the second, third length of pipe and somewhere after that everything came to a screeching halt as we struck what we believed to be a large rock, and rather than pulling up the pipe and starting all over, we gave up on a quest for water, continuing to bring out gallons of it from Detroit.

Now about the oil. There was a farmer just west of us, Mr. Bringle who led a rather frugal life style, barely eking out a living from his land, which included acreage behind our property. This was in the early 1980's when we witnessed an unusual amount of activity on his land behind us and came to find out that an oil crew was drilling, eventually finding oil but to our bad luck, we didn't have any share in it. All we could do was look at this well pumping oil day in and day out. It was the first oil well in Washtenaw County. We had earlier signed oil leases for drilling but no drilling took place in our land. By the way, we later heard that Mr. Bringle became arrogant and demanding as a result of his new found wealth.

It was early in 1983 as we were preparing for our daughter Catherine's wedding when we were approached by Mosbacher Oil Company out of Houston to sign an oil lease. We had been through this before and put their representative off stating we were in the middle of wedding plans and could he come back to see us after the wedding. The wedding was on a Saturday and the following Monday the oil company rep showed up at our door step to sign us up. Several months passed with no activity. One day I went out to the farm taking one of the graduate students with me. (More about the students will be discussed later on). To our surprise there was oil drilling going on and the news about finding oil was encouraging but would we share in it? Yes! The oil well was to cover 80 acres of land, including our ten acres. The well known as Tapp 5 was on the Bentley property behind their house, which gave them a 30-acre share in the royalty interest. Interests total 64 parts with 8 or 1/8 representing the royalty interest. This goes to the landowners free from expenses from income derived from the oil production. The remaining 7/8 or working interest bears the cost. An interesting side note, a man and his wife came out to meet us on the farm, offering us $10,000 for our oil interest but my husband and I decided that we had come this far and we would take our chances. This paid off for us as the first check, covering oil production for a short period of time came to us in the amount of $6,000 plus. It arrived in time for Christmas stockings, which had something extra for our girls and their mates, tickets to Ireland.

CHAPTER V

EXPERIENCE WITH OUR OVERSEAS STUDENTS.

From 1983 to 1986 we had the pleasure of having overseas students with graduate degrees stay with us. Their degrees were business related and they all belonged to a sponsoring organization know as ISAAC which was a world wide organization placing these graduate students in jobs with major corporations in most cases to practice their skills in their specialty fields. If the United

Now married, Marie ISAAC student from Austria. 2004

States took in, for example 3000 graduate students then our country could send 3000 of our students worldwide. The tour of duty lasted six months. Our first experience was with Frank Hartman who came from Germany, and he was the son we never had, spoke perfect English and was handsome beyond description. Frank went to work for North American Rockwell. I introduced Frank to a single nurse friend of mine, thinking that a certain chemistry would develop but later learned that Frank with his good looks would have no trouble attracting girl friends. Frank was meticulous, a German trait, and was so very clean, neat and helpful around the house. We learned early on that Frank loved two things, driving the Chrysler freeway like it was a German Autobahn and Southern Comfort whiskey. My husband packed a small bottle of Southern Comfort in his luggage when he returned home. Before Frank returned home we had a surprise party for him, inviting girl friends we knew of and surprisingly, they all got along with each other. The attendees included other ISAAC students, employees, friends, and more importantly, his girl friends he dated in the United States. We still correspond with Frank and we are not aware if he married his long time German girl friend.

We had a lovely young lady from Brazil named Lais, as our second guest. Lais met her husband to be, also from Brazil while with us and within she married him. She was a very gentle lady, and very cooperative with house rules, which really consisted of keeping her room neat, and removing her dishes from the table. We went for many walks together, in uptown Birmingham, which is only about one and a half miles from our home.

Marie Kastner, from Austria, was one of my favorites, as she was very vocal with me, which I loved. We were friendly foes, challenging each other and standing our ground. Her parents owned a resort in Austria. Marie had a very close friend named Petra from Germany. Petra stayed with

Now married, Petra, ISAAC student from Germany. 2005

my sister in law Helen Becker, and my niece Pamela Wilde nee Becker had one of the students from Ireland. We had three students then, so we were unable to take on anymore. Petra and Marie traveled together while here, to Canada, Boston, Washington DC and spent many weekends together; on their return to their countries they both eventually married and are now raising families. We just received a lovely letter from both ladies, and enclosed were pictures of their husbands and children. For a brief time we had Maeve from Ireland who moved on to rent a home with other ISAAC students.

Next student we had was Ann from Belgium, she was unique in the sense that she was raised in wealth. Her parents were both Doctors, and she never had to pick up after herself. My house rules were "I am not your maid". But I do have a cleaning lady weekly. She kept her room in disarray. Stella would spend about one hour in her room, until I said to her don't clean her room. One day she returned from work and said "Why was Stella not here today" I informed her that I do not pay Stella to just clean her room. We had a sit down talk with Ann and she got the message. From then on she was helpful.

My husband Jay took a special interest with all our students, taking them to fine restaurants, concerts, cooking gourmet meals for them.

While we enjoyed each and every one of our students, we were glad to have our house return to our home.

VACATION TIME

Vacations were always family affairs and generally involved renting a cottage on a lake. Black Lake in the northern part of the lower peninsula of Michigan was one of our favorites. It was close to Mackinac City as well as Petoskey with the manufacturers retail discount outlet stores and of course we could walk the beaches of Lake Michigan looking for the popular Petoskey stones. Michigan's state rock is the Petoskey stone.

We also vacationed in Leamington, Ontario, Canada on Lake Erie with another couple. Leamington's claim to fame was its acres and acres of

Julie & Jenny Washabaugh at The Hotel Europe in Kilarney, Ireland.

tomato farmland, which supplied the gigantic Heinz Company operation. Jay and our good friend Jack Schenk played golf every day at the Leamington golf course, home of major tournaments.

Another summer vacation was spent at nearby Lake Orion with two significant memories. The first was the location of our cottage, which was across the lake from Jimmy Hoffa's summer home. It was a gorgeous place covering at least three lots. The other memory was a temporary escape back home. (It wasn't that far from Lake Orion to our home). About half way back someone said, "Did we leave the kettle on?" We debated about continuing on and reluctantly turned back to find that we had pulled the plug on the kettle. From then on the question "Did we leave the kettle on" carried on our future trips. We deviated from lake vacations for two years in a row, heading over to Princeville, Ontario, Canada, near Owens Sound to a dude ranch called

Bootjack Ranch. The wife of the owner was the local doctor. Needless to say, we had a ball riding the horses each day and walking the trails followed with western style Bar-B-Q.'s.

Our first trip to Florida came in 1969, in the month of July in a 1965 Dodge Dart with no air conditioning. We solved that by being on the road at 6am and off at around 2pm enjoying pool and air conditioning at motels on the way down and back. We must have passed a million signs and billboards stating "See Ruby Falls" which we never did. The 1-75 freeway was still under construction at that time which meant that we had to get back on the old Dixie highway for 40 or 50 mile stretches on narrow two-lane road going through small towns. The town's people had their wares out by the road, hand made afghans and the like hoping that people would stop by and purchase some. We stayed with Jay's brother Francis and his wife Peggy who treated us like royalty, taking us to oyster bars, shelling on Mandalay Beach in Clearwater Beach. They had moved down to Clearwater in the early '60's and settled in what was the suburbs, which didn't last long as the Florida population exploded much to their dismay creating gridlock. They warned us to stay out of the midday sun, which we observed faithfully with one exception. Toward the end of our stay we took our daughters to a miniature golf course and part way through, Meg turned ashen white and Jay quickly picked her up and brought her into an air conditioned building which revived her. Lesson learned, don't deviate from fair warnings! Our trip back was eventful in the fact that when we arrived in the Cincinnati, Ohio area we listened to the historic description of Neil Armstrong's moon landing and walk. This only whetted our appetite to get home and turn on the TV to see the rerun of the landing.

We had one more trip to Florida by car and my husband reminded me of our stay in a small town in Georgia. We did our usual things using all the amenities, which came with the motel. We asked the desk clerk for directions to a good restaurant, not the usual chain type restaurant. Were we lucky! It turned out to be an antebellum mansion converted into a restaurant, owned and operated by two sisters who served up the best southern cooking we ever had. The atmosphere was simply elegant. Following our meal we asked one of the owners for directions to a Catholic Church which she provided. We turned down a street named Joe Louis Drive, which took us into the black area of the town. There sat the church, a simple cinder block building and we made it in time for the Saturday liturgy. The priest was from Ireland and we met and talked to him afterwards. We asked how big was his parish and he said it was 50 miles. Evidently not too many Catholics in that part of Georgia. We also asked if there were many black Catholics and his answer was rather profound as he said it was bad enough being black in the south but you had your own black relatives and friends to support you. But if you were black and Catholic you also lost your black support.

Again we stayed with my in-laws who again treated us like royalty. Future trips to Florida were made by plane. Francis died in 1978 from cancer at the age of 63 and a year later his wife Peggy died from what was described as heart failure, but I believe to this day that she just lost her will to live without Francis as they were like two peas in a pod.

HIGH SCHOOL GRADUATIONS

Both our daughters graduated from Mercy High School in Farmington Hills. While we had a big party for Meg for her 1976 graduation we decided to offer Cathy a trip for all of us to the French Riviera, or as the French called it. Cote d'Azur. We had instant takers. That was in 1977 and to this day we marvel

Brigitte with her children. Her parents Marie Anne, Roger Pradie, Jay's Cousin

at the super good deal we had as our basic cost for round trip air and luxury hotel in Cannes ran just under $2,000 for all four of us. This was a charter airline with about half going to Nice and the rest going to Rome. Our trip to the Riviera had some glitches and memories too. First off, our flight from JFK scheduled for 9 pm didn't leave until 2am due to the air controllers slow down in Northern Europe. Then there was the incident of the man who boarded the flight in New York who was inebriated. He demanded that the people in front of us give up their seats and eventually he was escorted off the plane. On the brighter side I met a man who had just checked himself out of a hospital, still wearing his wrist 1.D. band saying that if he was going to die it would be when he was having a good time on the Riviera. I happened to be sitting next to him, at that time I was working part time at the cardiac unit of a hospital and I asked him about his wrist band He was very casual about signing himself out of a cardiac care unit. I thought I took care of the likes of him all day and now here I am going on vacation with my family and a cardiac patient sits next to me. We arrived in the brilliant sunshine of Cote d'Azur, at the Nice airport. Flying into the Nice airport requires a dip over the Mediterranean Sea and flying in from the south into a narrow corridor. Once in Nice we proceeded by bus to Cannes and stayed at the glamorous Montfleury Hotel, where we were told that Elizabeth Taylor and Richard Burton stayed during the Cannes festival. Cannes is only a short distance from Nice where my husband's aunt Lucie lived. She was 88 years old. We met her three children, Madeline, Marie-Anne and her priest son, Jean Stahl. Madeline never married but Marie—Anne married Roger Pradie and had one daughter, Brigitte. Lucie spoke English but after all those years would slip back into French. She was very reflective of her trip to America during the mid-20's expecting to stay in America.

Jay's uncle Lucien had settled in Portland, Oregon and tried to entice Lucie, Rene and family to settle there promising housing and other amenities which never materialized. Disappointed they all returned home. Lucie to her native France where she eventually married Leon Stahl.

Lucie Adele was the youngest in the family, born in1888. She graduated from the Conservatory of Strasbourg and was a gifted violinist. Lucie passed her love of music on to her children with Madeline majoring in piano, Marie-Anne in violin at the Conservatory of Strasbourg while her son Jean Stahl majored in organ at the Paris Conservatory. When I first met Lucie she was in bed as she had severe back problems. I gave her a back rub and she was so very happy about this. Having lived through two world wars, she had bitter memories of her life under the Hitler regime. Following the invasion and take over of France by the Nazis in World War11, her son was forced into the German Luftwaffe under threat of concentration camp for all. Meanwhile learning of her and her children's musical abilities, the Nazis directed them to perform concerts for the occupation troops. Aunt Lucie stated that all the German troops wanted to hear was German music, shouting "We want to hear Mozart" pronouncing the name with a hard "Z" and she would pronounce Mozart with a soft "Z", saying Qui, Mozart" just to antagonize the occupation forces. She also relayed to us that all the people had to fill out extensive genealogy forms to find out if there were any Jews in their background history. Fortunately for them, they had a long background of Christian history going back to the early 1700's.

Her son Jean entered the priesthood in a remarkable way. Aboard a troop train heading for the Russian front, the train made a stop in Paris. He knew Paris like the back of his hand and somehow managed to slip out of the train but his absence was soon detected and the Gestapo went after him in hot pursuit. He eluded them, escaping through various back alleys. With the help of friends who sheltered him he came out of hiding to find work as an organist at a tiny Paris radio station. Another close call was to happen.

1999. With my brother Deny on his farm.

While performing he was alerted to the arrival of the Gestapo looking for him, and he barely escaped slipping out one door as the Gestapo charged in with guns drawn. He took refuge in a monastery outside of Paris, staying there for the duration of the war.

The Nazis then kept a 24-hour watch on his mom's home. She was repeatedly warned and threatened that if she ever held back any information about her son's whereabouts she would be put in a concentration camp along with the rest of the family. Jean Stahl of course had the sense to remain silent, never contacting her but it had to be a gut wrenching experience for her not knowing if he was dead or alive. It was with great relief when the war ended that her son was found safe. This was hard on my husband's family, as they had no idea if Lucie and her family was alive. With the good news that all had survived, my husband's family sent over food and clothing to their French relatives.

Jean meanwhile was ordained into the priesthood and in communication with his family learned that he wanted my father in law's music for organ. He also was in desperate need for shoes. The music was sent over to him as well as a pair of military brogans. How he was ever able to play the organ and do intricate pedal work with those heavy and wide shoes was a mystery to all. For a good part of our stay in Cannes, my husband traveled to Nice by train to spend time with his aunt while we toured around the Cote d'Azur. We were attracted to all the tourist traps including the nude beaches. Hated to leave the Riviera as each day was an adventure with so many things to do and see. My husband who spent much time with his aunt Lucie in Nice knew or sensed that this would be the last trip to see his Aunt Lucie.

At the nude beach at San Tropez I walked up to an elderly man and asked him why he wore a beret and nothing more. He said he wore it to keep his head from becoming sun burned. So much for French logic. One goes from the French Riviera to the Italian Riviera, passing by Monaco. We didn't stop at Monaco although my husband had two years earlier done so, winning at the slots. The temptation to buy leather goods such as shoes, purses was irresistible as it is better than going to the duty free shops at the airport but one has to remember, you don't take the opening price for anything as it becomes a bargaining session. One thing we did not bargain for was a shop owner who offered his son to our daughter

My dad with my daughters, Catherine and Margaret.

Cathy in marriage. This caught us off guard and all we could do was sputter something like thanks but no thanks. Aside from this, it was a glorious time visiting the Italian Riviera.

One of the things that make parents age is allowing our 19 and 17 year old daughters to roam free on their own. After we had rested from our very long flight from Detroit to the Riviera, the girls decided to check out the Mediterranean Sea and came upon a group of young people setting to go on a yacht. Our daughters were invited to join in and of course, they did. Gone several hours we became concerned. The true meaning of joy and relief was to find them return, safe and sound. Naturally, they thought nothing about this as young people do. We were sure this time would be our last time to see them alive. It was a very emotional experience for all of us. Flying out of the Nice airport you immediately find yourself over the Mediterranean Sea, flying to Rome to pick up the rest of the tourists. What happened to us going to the Riviera happened again at the Rome airport, only worse.

Left to right: Jenny, Rosemary Kelleher, Julie & Cathy, 1999.

Beckers' Home, 1993. Doris & George Ball. Sheila & Meg, Linda & John Gagliadi.

The air controllers in Northern Europe, still on a slow down mode, caused all the flights to be delayed or canceled. The airport in Rome ran out of food, drinks etc. and it was very hot, causing people to become angry. We were resigned to stay at the Rome airport for hours but as luck would have it, a Pan Am flight was on the runway for hours and the crew decided to walk off which left an opening for our flight to move into their slot. The original flight plan for our departure, which would take us over Switzerland, was changed and went over France, past Paris at night. Paris, the City of Lights was awesome. We landed at the Shannon airport in the early morning hours for refueling. This gave us an hour or so to shop at the duty free shops but more importantly it gave me a chance to call all my family members with local calls. No one complained getting up to answer the phone in the middle of the night.

We arrived back at JFK too late to catch our connecting flight and had to wait another couple of hours to connect to another flight back to Detroit. It's times like this that one learns the true meaning of being tired. We could have kissed the ground when we arrived back to our home and beds.

TRIPS TO IRELAND

I have been back to Ireland more times than I can remember, returning first in1962 with my two daughters, Meg and Kit. First off I was accused of losing my brogue and my daughters were referred to as the little Yanks. My mother had earlier died so we visited at the family residence, the old family farm, which still needed the basic amenities, my husband was used to.

My father had mellowed quite a bit by this time. Meg and Kit had a great time chasing the pigs that in turn chased them. They loved to roam about in the fields. Returning home was another situation. My family got us to the airport too late and the three of us and four others, unrelated, missed our flight back home. Jay went to the airport to meet us and was more than surprised to hear him paged to come to the Delta counter where he was met by the tour organizer informing him of what had happened but not to worry as we were put on another flight, which was diverted from Paris to Shannon to pick us up. We made it home late but OK.

As a family member we finally convinced Jay to come to Ireland but only after he was assured that we would have all the modern day conveniences. The first trip resulted from our oil well bonanza and we spent three weeks in Ireland, mainly in a rented home on the Dingle Peninsula. Fishing was one of the high lights for the males and of course touring the ring of Kerry and other sights filled in the gaps between relatives dropping in to visit. We did have one narrow escape caused by a tire that blew out. There's hardly a place to pull off in the narrow Irish roads, because of the hedges or stonewalls but we managed to pull into a driveway and change the tire. The tire itself was a total disgrace, completely bald, no tread what so ever. Jay put on the spare, which was hardly much better and at the nearest garage bought a new tire. Needless to say the rental people heard about this incident with much detail. My husband and I returned to Ireland for two weddings, one in Killarney and the other in a remote church in County Cork. The one in Killarney was at the magnificent Cathedral, while the other reminded us of the play "Brigadoon" as we drove along with nothing but country scenery and suddenly there it was in the middle of nowhere, this tiny decades if not centuries old church about the size of a chapel. My husband made the wry remark, "0.K, where are the leprechauns?"

October, 1993. Sister, Nora O'Leary and Denny with my sister Theresa to my right.

Our most recent trip was back home as a family took place in 1999. Three generations of us were there and we stayed at the Hotel Europe in Killarney, making this our headquarters for all my family members to visit us. The Hotel Europe is a five star hotel, owned and operated by Germans located in the outskirts of Killarney on acres of land beautifully groomed. All the conveniences were available including horse back riding and golf courses. This time we rented a van and our daughter Meg did the driving with Kit providing directions. My nephew Jerry came over from Millstreet several times taking over the driving chores as we visited all the usual places near and around Killarney.

We managed to get over to Millstreet for Sunday mass and we were surprised to see a coffin up near the altar. Yes, we were told, the churches in the smaller towns and rural areas still held on the practice of funerals on Sunday.

We went out to lunch after mass and then back to my old home outside Millstreet where my brother Denis lived, tending his herd of milk cows. It was to be the last time I would see Denis alive as in 2001, he suffered a stroke and finally passed on in March of 2001. It was also the last time I would see my sister Nora O'Leary who was living in Killarney and visited us there at our hotel. We learned that she had just gotten out of the hospital following cancer surgery but didn't say a word to us. It was only after she left our room did her daughter Etta inform me of the details.

We managed to see some of our friends who after many years in America moved back to Ireland and in one case we met one of Meg's friends, Mary Tobin, an American of Irish descent who retired from her job at the University of Michigan and decided to move over, partly due to someone she expected to marry, but it never took place for various reasons. Mary, as it turned out is more Irish than the Irish.

Back to Shannon for our return flight back home. The flight was delayed four and a half hours caused by a warning device, which indicated some type of mechanical problems. As it turned out, the warning device was the problem and I think that to this day that perhaps this was man made to have us spend more money at the duty free shops!

OTHER TRIPS

One of our favorite trips, usually by car, was going down to Virginia Beach to visit my sister Joan and her husband Dr. Jack McSweeney. The game plan was always the same, go as far as Hagerstown, Maryland and check in at the Ramada Inn with all it's amenities including a superb restaurant called "Tortuga" which is Spanish for turtle. We had an encounter with an actual turtle on one of our trips while riding on the

1993—Tom Washabaugh, son-in-law, my Nephew Neil O'Driscoll and wife Enda.

Pennsylvania turnpike. The girls yelled watch it dad, there's a turtle crossing the turnpike!

Thump, thump followed by complete silence. The warning came too late and we never heard the last of it. Our Kit graduated from Michigan Tech with a degree in Geological Engineering in June 1982 and was soon engaged to marry her college friend Tom Washabaugh.

Figuring this would be our last family trip we set off for the east coast to Virginia Beach then down the coast into Charleston, South Carolina where we stayed overnight. Jay and the girls checked with the locals for a nice seafood restaurant. Checking with the locals was by this time a standard practice and it paid off again as we sat at tables spread with newspapers to catch the shells from peel and eat shrimp, Alaskan crab legs, oysters, cat fish and whatever else you could name for under $10 each and oh, it was all you could eat too. We eventually arrived in Florida then back home via 1-75.

1999—Ring of Kerry. Jenny, Cathy & Julie.

My son in law Tom Washabaugh's family consisted of five boys and two girls. The girls were the first in over 80 years as recorded in their genealogy chart. We had our two daughters, Meg and Kit and as my husband always said. "We went for quality, not quantity" the Washabaugh children were all quality and I say this as they reflect on Tom's parents, Bill and Norma. Family trips for them were always in an R/V and it seemed like every couple of years the R/V got bigger and bigger. This leads now to another trip to Virginia Beach for the wedding of Joan and Jack's daughter Rosemary.

My nephew, Jerry Kelleher from Ireland had come over here for the summer and when we heard that a newer R/V, the size of a bus had been delivered to Tom's parents that we would all travel down for the wedding. The R/V was dropped off for maintenance at a Bay City auto shop a month before the wedding and it was expected that it would be tuned up and ready to go in time.

Well, it wasn't. Panic set it, calls back and forth between Bay City and Birmingham confirmed that the shop had not even touched it but was only working on it now.

We waited all night for Tom, Kit to arrive and they finally did, at the break of dawn. The R/V was as big as we thought it would be. To talk to someone from the back you had to get on the telephone.

We settled back for the long journey down, this time making no stops in Hagerstown but driving straight through. Tom would get the R/V up over 50 miles per hour and it would kick back as if there was a governor on it and as a result we could not make good time going down to Virginia Beach and when we arrived, the night before the wedding, we missed out not only on the wedding rehearsal dinner but a surprise birthday party for me. We did survive and oh yes, managed to get someone to look at the R/V. and found the gas line had been pinched cutting off the fuel line which was the cause of the problem.

We must remember our friends and others by bringing up the next stories. Our friend Jack was best man at our wedding and my husband was his best man a year later at his wedding. We have been in touch with him over the years. To begin with Jack moves around a lot as evidenced with an examination of his true resume. If his resume of jobs were to be printed here it would fill the rest of the book. His marriage lasted 18 years and ended in tragedy. His wife had mental problems which he said he could deal with but she hallucinated back in Atlanta, Georgia by not taking her medications, using alcohol, and driving off in the car, going down the wrong side of the road, ran into a car, killing three young girls, and permanently putting the only survivor in a wheel chair for life.

2001—Pumpkin party, South Lyon, Michigan.

Divorce followed and we still correspond with his ex-wife. Jack remarried and he and his wife Mary have been blissfully happy.

We have visited them in Texas and hope to see them now in Las Vegas, Nevada. Jack remains the same, a butterfly that thinks he can always get a job and the truth is, he does!

Now, on to our friends, Hank and Wanda Baczynski. Wanda was married to Tony Krist who died very young from lung cancer. Some years later she married Hank who was an engineer, making lots of money running a plant in Jackson, Michigan. We visited once or twice a year and eventually Henry retired. After some years Hank and Wanda moved out to Las Vegas, Nevada. With his position as an engineer for a large company we always thought he was well healed but we learned later on that this was not so.

Their house back in Michigan sold for much less than anyone expected and evidently Hank and Wanda went through whatever money they had. We went out to Las Vegas to visit them. It was a sad reunion. While in Jackson, Michigan we visited them at least annually taking them out for dinner at their favorite restaurant located at the airport. Shortly after our visit in late 1998 or there about, Hank died and Wanda was placed in a nursing home. Hank designed our two seater out house on the farm. Wanda is the sister of my husband's sister-in-law, Helen.

My brother Pat was trained as an auto mechanic back in Ireland and came over in the 1950's settling in San Francisco working for Checker Cab Company. Eventually he obtained an ownership interest in the cab company. Pat and his wife Eileen have two children, Margaret Mary and Denis. Eileen was one of the best things that ever happened to my brother, as she was very instrumental in helping him stop his drinking. She is also very clever in the business world, as they both bought up many acres of land in Ireland many years ago, and today he has profited well from this investment. My brother never informed me that he owned any land. However, during my many trips to Ireland my sister Theresa showed me the many acres of land that belonged to my brother. Real estate in California must be sold by the inch, as the houses are tall, straight up and basically no room between them plus very little back yard. He, his wife Eileen and Margaret flew here for our daughters Cathy's wedding in 1983 and while sitting in our back patio all he could say was," Jesus Christ! If I owned your house I would build two more houses in you back yard." This was the only time he visited us, but every year he has promised to come by train etc. But we went to Metro airport several times to see them, when they were on their way to Virginia Beach to visit my sister Joan who at that time had terminal cancer, they stayed down there for two weeks. Metro airport is the hub for Northwest Airlines. Coax as we would, he and Eily never spent a day with us.

On the other hand, we traveled to California on a number of occasions, spending time with them. There is one memory at least to share. Pat in all his years never bought a used or new car, but one he would take home from checker cab, which was his mode of travel. One Sunday morning he drove Eileen to mass and she was outside the church after mass waiting for him, and overheard one lady saying "there is someone out there who keeps circling, driving an ugly dark green car". When Eily heard this she knew who the lady was talking about, and when she got home, read the riot act to my brother who then went out and bought a decent car. My brother Pat, who I love dearly, never kissed the Blarney stone, he swallowed it! It took me a long time to wake up to the fact that he was as dumb as a fox. When I was in Ireland he never told anyone that he was dating his wife Eileen, and it was only recently that I learned that it was my sister Kate who was a nurse in the hospital where his wife worked introduced them. Now today my daughter Cathy and his daughter Margaret Mary meet once a year at a SPA, just inside of Mexico, south of San Diego, to spend a week of luxury treatment.

MEMORIES OF GEORGE AND DORIS BALL AS WELL AS LILLY AND SHAFI

First of all George and Doris Ball became our life long friends. I met George at his son Tim's wedding Doris did not attend. Their son Tim married into my son-in-laws family the Washabaugh's. I will never forget that wedding, as I had to keep begging George to dance with me. I introduced him to my husband and from then on they became great friends. I finally met his wife Doris who then was a fully licensed psychologist in uptown Birmingham. She spent hours helping me with my psychological testing, as then I was a student psychologist down at The Center For Humanistic Studies not doing well with my testing.

My daughter Cathy refers to the Balls as her second parents, as they wine and dine her every time she travels to that Mexican based spa, Rancho La Puerta just south of San Diego in Mexico. George is a retired nuclear physicist from Detroit Edison, while Doris is a retired teacher and later on a psychologist. They researched the country to find a place which would be the best for them to escape the problems associated with allergies, and whatever, finding San Diego the ideal area to avoid all these nasty problems. To some degree that helped, but it seems that other ailments developed, and who knows, maybe George and Doris are just sitting back with herbal and other remedies to attack the next to come ailments.

Doris was born in Sault Ste. Marie, Canada. She lost a daughter, Debbie in a horrible car accident. Debbie was on her way to school when she was struck by a car. At any age, child, teen or older, it is a terrible loss. We understand her hurt and think back often to this tragic event.

Our friends Lilly and Shafi were introduced to us by some friends. Shafi was working for Volkswagen and he and Lilly were on their way to Hong Kong where Shafi was assigned. Lilly was in our back yard talking about being told to buy shoes here in America before traveling to Hong Kong because they were very expensive over there. By coincidence, I had just brought back several pairs of shoes, never worn and owned by our son-in-laws grandmother, brought them out and found they were a perfect fit. We were to meet again in Hong Kong as one day my husband said" Would you like to visit Hong Kong?" I thought he was kidding but not so. Northwest Airlines had just started a Detroit to Hong Kong flight and as an introductory price came out with a Hong Kong-Detroit flight round trip, two nights at the Holiday Inn on the Golden Mile of Hong Kong, half day tour of Hong Kong, all for $700 each.

At that time it was not a direct flight but a stop over in Seattle to pick up a Boeing 747. By the time we arrived in Hong Kong we had gone through 13 time zones, leaving on a Tuesday morning and arriving in Hong Kong Wednesday at around 6pm. As we checked through customs my husband said he didn't know if he should say, "good morning" or "good evening, following 18 hours travel time.

It was here we met up with Shafi and Lilly who were living in Kowloon, across the water from Hong Kong. Volkswagen put them up in a luxury apartment, about 1100 square feet at a monthly rental of $6000. We learned early on that real estate was pricey. For example if you want to be buried in Hong Kong, the burial plot cost $45,000. A hotel making a bottom line net profit of $ 60 million was torn down to build a high rise office building which would more than double the hotel's net profit. At the time we were there, in 1994, Hong Kong was still under British rule and you could feel the tense anticipation of the Chinese take over. We were glad we went when we did and would think twice before returning. While there we visited a residence for British naval personnel, which was the home of Forbes McDonald, brother of one of our neighbors here in Michigan. Forbes had died earlier but we wanted to see where he lived and returned with pictures for his sister, Lillian who lived by our home. One of the exciting things was to meet up with Joe and LaVerne Smith. Joe is the brother of Henry who was married to my husband's sister Catherine. We knew they were coming over and waited for them in their hotel, much to their surprise, here we were, Joe and my husband, born in Alton, Illinois, meeting half way around the world. We did all the tourist things during our stay and avoided all the street merchants selling "Rolex' watches and other cheap imitation items.

Returning to the states was much faster than our trip over to Hong Kong as we had a jet stream tail wind to help us along. By the way, flying in and out of Hong Kong is about an exciting an event you would ever want to experience. With the new airport all this is lost but the old airport meant one actually flew between tall buildings to get in and out of Hong Kong.

Because of the International dateline we arrived back in Seattle four hours before we left Hong Kong and had to wait for customs personnel to show up, returning in the early morning hours. For Jay, this was a mission accomplished as he had planned to travel to Hong Kong when he was stationed in Japan during The Korean War. The fellow airman he planned to travel with was busted for stealing a camera thus ending their planned trip. Jay also said, after climbing Mt. Fuji that there was a Japanese saying which went this way: One is foolish not to climb Mt. Fuji once in a lifetime and twice as foolish to climb it a second time. We both felt this was true of Hong Kong, nice to go once but not twice.

Shafi and Lily returned to Michigan a few months later, spending some time with us. Jay took Shafi with him to pick up a bunch of concert tickets for a Rackham Choir concert and introduced Shafi to the owner of the print shop by saying, "This is Shafi, who was born in India, is a Canadian citizen, lives in Germany and now is on his way to Hong Kong. The print shop owner responded, "Who is he running away from"? We have very interesting friends

BACK IN IRELAND

My brother Denis, who never married, lived in our old house in Claraghatlea, just outside Millstreet. Over the years the house was modernized with updated conveniences but inside it had a monastic appearance, very plain and simple. His life style was that way too, plain and simple. Denny had a dairy herd of cows and because of this was restricted to staying on the farm and as his needs were simple, he would drive into town for his daily food needs or wind up at my sister's house for dinner. Driving a car, which was well over 20 years old, the Irish government contacted him with a monetary offer that he could not refuse to encourage him to buy a newer car. We learned this on our family trip to Ireland in 1999.

Denny was fortunate to live close to my sister Theresa who cared for him like a mother through illness or whatever. Denny suffered a mild stroke in early 2001and later in March, had a second and more severe stroke. I had many phone calls back and forth with his family.

However as usual I never received the correct information as my nephew notified me by email saying "Your brother is now doing so well he will be starting speech therapy and physical therapy next week." I had the intuition that all was not well as I recalled ten years earlier when my sister Kate, diagnosed with cancer was doing well, only to find out that it wasn't true and she refused to have any additional treatment. She died soon after and I was informed that she did not want to worry us.

Millstreet Library, Breda O'Leary-Librarian, County Cork, Ireland. 2001

So the hectic plans began with our daughter Meg and my husband working fever- ishly to get me on a plane to Ireland, we found a flight to Shannon via Air Lingus through Chicago. Of course when you are flying on a domestic airline to an International airline, they are at opposite ends of the airport. Usually my hus- band is traveling with me and handles all the details but this time I had to do it on my own, and success-

fully I might add, got over to the O'Hare International Air terminal. Meanwhile, back home, Jay was notified with the sad news that Denny had expired, and I was to find this out when I arrived at the Shannon airport by my nephew's wife Agnes O'Driscoll.

She drove me to her husband's university where he teaches close to their home. Then he drove me down to Millstreet. However this time returning home for my brother's funeral was a different experience for me. I called my wonderful brother-in-law Tadhg and asked him if I could stay with him. I knew my sister Theresa was overwhelmed with taking care of my brother Denis's funeral arrangements so I stayed with Tadhg. He was just great to me as he gave me the key to his home so I was able to come and go as I pleased. I spent my days mainly at the library as they had a computer there. I spent the majority of my time doing research in the library.

The librarian Brenda O' Leary was more than helpful to me with using email. Many times I asked her for help and not once did she say "No I am unable to do that now" as she willingly left whatever she was doing and came over to my desk where the computer was. This was following my brother's funeral at St. Patrick's Church in Millstreet.

Ireland does things differently from what I have now been accustomed to in America. When I viewed my brother's remains, it was at the hospital morgue. Eventually he was brought to the church for the funeral and following the funeral I stood in line with other family members, as the mourners walked by to shake our hands, offering condolences. I thought my hand would never recover from all the handshakes, until my nephew Jerry Kelleher said to me "Turn that ring around" and it no longer hurt. We and many others dined afterwards in typical Irish fashion. We had a great lunch, with soup, salad, and any kind of meat sandwich that one could ask for. This was served in a bar across the street from where I stayed with my brother-in-law Tadhg O'Driscoll.

2001. Sitting with Jerry Kelleher and his mom, my sister Theresa Kelleher with Sean Radley's pictorial history of Millstreet.

During my stay in Ireland I had time on my hands because I had booked the return flight over ten days, expecting of course that I would see Denny while still alive. I was very lucky as I met a gentleman named Sean Radley who is a native of Millstreet. From the first time he saw, at the age of eight, a historic picture of his beloved town as it was in (C.1910) he developed a life long interest in preserving and recording the ongoing history of the area. In 1978, he was among the founding members of the Millstreet Museum Society.

Now, as the Millstreet Museum Curator he has been responsible for the publication of a variety of local color postcards, for contributing updates on museum development to local media, for the presentation of a number of local radio programs relating to Millstreet and for the coordination of historic tours of the area. Sean helped to organize quite a few thematic exhibitions at The Museum Center in Millstreet's Carnegie Hall.

Sean is uplifted by the positive response and encouragement he receives from a wide range, cross section wise, of local people in relation to the work being carried out at both the Museum and the Tourist Information Center. It was this inspiring support, which contributed to the motivation to compile and publish "Picture Millstreet" Profile of Millstreet 1880-1980. This book is a pictorial history of Millstreet for the one hundred years it covers and has many pictures of my family members and others I grew up with. Presently Millstreet now has its own Web Site, thanks to Mr. Radley and I have personally benefited from this, in contacting people who were born in Ireland and now living all throughout the world, through the internet. My ten days in Ireland were eventful in another way. It was the height of the mad cow disease as well as the hoof and mouth disease. Communities in rural areas such as Millstreet were on full alert combating the spread of these dread diseases. You could not go into any public building without first stepping on a large sponge filled with disinfectant. Since I spent many hours at the library, daily my shoes were disinfected. Fortunately my area was not affected but regardless, the government was taking no chances.

Returning to America and landing at O'Hare Airport in Chicago, I discovered that the Americans were equally careful about the animal disease in Europe. For those who spent their time in major cities, they were whisked through quickly but a few, including me, who had been in the countryside of Ireland were detained and placed in a separate area. Each and every one of us were sniffed by dogs before being allowed to move on to connecting flights. The delay nearly cost me missing my flight back to Detroit. Compounding matters, violent rainstorms in the Chicago area caused planes to be diverted to other cities including Detroit, which resulted in all the American Airline gates to be fully occupied, by these planes and we had to wait after landing until a gate would be opened.

Looking back now I am glad I went as I really loved my brother, and I wanted to see things for myself. The Irish have caught up with the Americans in many ways, both good and bad. There is now full employment, free education including university training, home ownership has surged, all sorts of technical advances, high taxes, on and on. There is gridlock caused by too many cars traveling on the same narrow roads and parking is desperate. The government is slowly reacting to these problems by building belt line roads skirting many of the small towns and attempting to encourage travel by rail but this all takes time. Also, the Church has lost much of its power, vocations are down, and there are problems similar to ours in the U.S., i.e., drugs, crime, and unwed mothers, to mention only a few things.

The book I brought back from Ireland, 'PICTURE MILLSTREET" and 'PHOTOGRAPHIC PROFILE OF MILLSTREET 1880-1980 contains the memories of my early days in Ireland. I do get unusual gut feelings as I examine these pictures, feelings of awe, sadness, and joy, spending many hours viewing these pictures. There is always something new that I missed seeing before. Seeing the picture of my brother Pat, taken in 1950 when he was training as an auto mechanic at the famous "Coleman Brother's Garage", located in the north end of Millstreet is memorable and remarkably the garage is still there. Then I see pictures of other brothers and sisters growing up in Millstreet, also our teachers and the children I grew up with. The mode of travel then was" the horse and trap" seen in many of the pictures, bringing home the turf which reminded me of the many hours I had to work in the bog. Being together with my brothers and sisters were generally happy times and I try to forget the negative experiences. Then there are pictures of Saint Patrick Church at the west end, and the beautifully maintained Presentation Convent attached to the Church, historic Drishane with its 15th century castle and impressive grounds are all still there to see and visit.

CHAPTER VI

ODDS AND ENDS
GOING ON VACATION WITH OUR GRANDCHILDREN

We have taken the grandchildren many places such as Niagara Falls, and the highlight of our trip was going near the falls in a boat with the water streaming down. The grandchildren really had a great time enjoying the majestic scenery. As we passed each interesting inlet the guide would explain the history of various places. We have many pictures of our trip to Niagara Falls. I will never forget the trip on the boat we took on Niagara River. We had to closely watch the girls, since they refused to stand in one place on that boat. Every time I looked for them they were already at the other end of the ship.

We went by train once to Toronto and took games to play with the girls. This was a time when Julie was just 5 years old and was unwilling to realize that she cannot win all the games. Grandpa was playing with her and she did not win. She was upset and said, "When I play with my dad he lets me win all the games" However when we returned home I asked her dad and he denied this. Time went fast on the train going but on returning we were delayed about four to five hours because of a fatal bicycle accident. We did have plenty of other games, coloring books, reading books for their age, and puzzles to amuse the children

On our last trip with the girls to Canada their mom kept reminding us "Be careful as there are three generations traveling with you. We took them to the Science Center in Toronto with its hands on experiments. We saw the butterfly exhibit at Niagara Falls and large signs warning, "Do not touch the butterflies" Well our little Jenny did not touch them however one did land on her finger and we took a lovely picture of it. The signs were not intended for the butterflies! The employees were very nice to her and simply wiped the butterfly off her finger.

Julie and Jenny are very close together and now that they are no longer babies. They have developed skills, which they enjoy together such as swimming. They also compete in math competitions up in Bay City when the final games were played, both girls were in a different buildings. To their mom's delight, they each finished first in their respective age groups and received gold medals.

BECKERS MUSIC REVIVED HERE IN MICHIGAN

It all started innocently with an article about Rene L. Becker appearing in the November 2000 issue of The American Organist, which was read by the editor of de Orgelvriend, a Dutch publication similar to The American Organist. The editor, Gerco Schaap contacted my husband to reprint the article in Dutch and asked if he was aware that Rene Becker's First Organ Sonata in G minor was recorded in the Netherlands in 1985 on LP and later, in 1991 put on CD. The performer was Willem Zwart. His son, Everhard Zwart recorded this sonata in Paris in 1999. This came as a complete surprise to my husband who was thrilled beyond belief to hear the news. The Dutch translation appeared in the March 2001 of de Orgelvriend and between the two articles we received much correspondence asking for music of my husband's father and even correspondence from a former pupil of his uncle Lucian in Portland, Oregon.

We learned that Willem Zwart obtained a copy of the First Organ Sonata in the1980's while on a concert tour in California. My father-in-law wrote over 400 compositions for organ, piano, violin, choral and liturgical works with over 100 of them published. This has been a true revival of his music, which can only be described as breath taking. Demand for his music in European circles has been unrelenting and sources indicate an entire CD will be devoted to his musical works.

Subsequent to the above we learned that Everhard would be in the United States to accompany a Dutch choral group in October 2001.

My husbands parents, Angela and Rene' with children Catherine, Rene' Claude and Francis. My husband was born 14 years after Francis.

My Husband's Father Professor Rene' Becker.

October, 2001. Jay Becker & Everhard Zwart from the Netherlands with Jay's Dads music on stand. First Organ Sonata in G Minor, Op.40.

There was a possibility that he could appear in concert here in Detroit between appearances with the choral group. This all faded away when the most ideal venues, Blessed Sacrament Cathedral and Holy Name Church in Birmingham were unavailable due to both churches undergoing major renovation work. Not to be outdone we planned to attend the choral concert in Grand Rapids, Michigan with our two daughters and two grand daughters, three generations of Rene Becker

The organizer of the tour for the choral group contacted us and said he would ask Everhard to play some of Rene Becker's music at the concert.

It should be mentioned that the entire concert tour was almost derailed with the September 11 terrorist attacks in New York City and Washington, D.C. as a few of the 90 member choral group pulled out of the tour including the choir director!

Everhard took control and both directed and accompanied the choir.

To a standing room audience the tour director and emcee introduced all of us just prior to Everhard's playing of Rene Becker's Prelude and Toccata from the First Organ Sonata, mentioning this was a first time experience for all of us, hearing it played in a live performance. This turned out to be a humbling experience to thundering applause.

We took Everhard Zwart back to our home with my husband giving him several copies of my father-in-law's music. Also, he was taken to the Cathedral hopeful of seeing the interior of the Cathedral and the Casavant organ but due to the renovations going on he only saw the exterior. We left as good friends, taking him to Greenfield Village where he met up with the Dutch choral group to continue on with the tour into Canada It is Everhard's desire to make an entire Becker CD., and wants to make the recording here in Detroit. The Becker musical revival is in full swing.

October 2001. Julie & Jenny at the Grand Rapids concert. Their great grandfather's music in the background.

Grand Daughters with my Husband at the Five Manual Organ, Grand Rapids, Michigan. Note Music is the First Organ Sonata by Rene' Becker.

HANDEL'S MESSIAH AND RACKHAM SYMPHONY CHOIR

Messiah, Handel's most successful and best-known oratorio, was composed in just 24 days from August 22 to September 14, 1741. It was first performed on April 13, 1742, during a charity concert in Dublin, Ireland, with Handel conducting. During the first London performance at Covent Garden Theatre in March, 1743, King George II started to his feet just as the first notes of the Hallelujah Chorus sounded. Since no subject of the King can remain seated while his monarch stands, the entire audience rose with him. Thus began a tradition.

A Detroit tradition is the annual performance of this master work by the Rackham Symphony Choir at Christmas time. Every year the question is, "Can it get any better?" Well, It does. More recently Rackham premiered "Too Hot To Handel", a gospel/jazz version of this oratorio and is now performed at the Detroit Opera House.

My husband has been involved with Rackham for a quarter of a century and because of this, we too, our entire family has participated in many ways as ushers, ticket takers etc. for not only Messiah but all concerts. Rackham founded in 1949 has performed with all the major orchestras in metro Detroit as well as Canada.

I bring this story out as I am so proud of the fact that it was the Irish who first heard Handel's Messiah!

University of Detroit
"Commencement" May 15, 1982

PERSONAL GROWTH

What someday might be a sequel to this book is the story of my personal growth, which was encouraged by my husband and children. I was lucky, as when the children were growing up I did not have to work full time. I worked every other weekend and our two daughters had a great time with their dad. They bonded well.

When the children were in high school I returned to school, attending the University of Detroit to obtain two degrees, which were Bachelor of Social Work and Masters in Guidance and Counseling. Then, I went on to the Center for Humanistic Studies to obtain a Psychology Specialist Degree. It was in the midst of this that I learned that I had ovarian cancer. This was in 1990. For me, I was one of the lucky ones as my cancer was encapsulated which meant that it was in a specific place and had not spread to the surrounding areas.

I hold a deep regard for Dr. Clark Moustakas and Dr. Cereta Perry at CHS who guided me through this development period. They continued to support and guide me in my next five years to obtain a Doctorate Degree in Clinical Psychology at the Union Institute University in Cincinnati, Ohio.

I conclude now by saying, "thank you all" for being a part of my life in my trip from Ireland to America.

Left to right: Sister In law Eileen O'Sullivan, Margaret Mary O'Sullivan, Sheila Becker and brother Patrick O'Sullivan. Mid 1990's.

San Francisco, May 2004. Family at the Everhard Zwart Concert

IRISH POEM

The following poem was written by:
Ms. Lil O' Connor
(a close friend)

With a tear for dear old Ireland
my beloved Emerald Isle
I pledged allegiance to America and
met its challenge with a smile

Though I had worked and studied
in my home across the seas
in Ireland and England progressing by degrees
'til at last I came here
to these United States
and finally to Detroit guided by my fates

I can not relate all I have learned O'er
the years of knowledge obtained, I can
only feel great appreciation, and love, for
friends, I have gained.

I now am a better person
more understanding of self and others,
with a high frustration tolerance,
toward my friends and loving brothers.

Gained imagination and creativeness,
Intuition and perception too
Free floating attention, with kindness,
and a genuine will to do.

So that though the rest of my life,
Though I travel far and wide, I shall
feel sweet contentment
And a peace inside.

PLEASE CALL ME SHEILA

BY SHEILA O'SULLIVAN BECKER

July 2005

*Dedicated to my two children,
Catherine Angela Washabaugh and
Margaret Mary Becker*

Meg, Cathy dressed for a
Rackham Concert

INTRODUCTION

I wrote my first book, _My Dream From Ireland To America_ in the hopes that it would inspire my grandchildren to work hard to become anything they want to be. I had to jump through many hoops to achieve my goals, but that made attaining them all the more special. It is my sincere hope that my first book, and now this one, will help teach my grandchildren that much of the satisfaction in realizing a dream comes along the way, on the road you took to get there.

I published _My Dream From Ireland To America_ myself for about $2000 at American Speedy Printers in Birmingham. The selling price was $15 per book, with the proceeds going to the St. Joseph Mercy Pontiac breast cancer support group in Pontiac. It has been gratifying for me to learn from St. Joseph's that the book has generated additional donations beyond the proceeds from readers who were moved to send in their own contribution.

My Dream From Ireland To America seemed to take forever and a day to write, fifteen years to be exact. I thought that was it, but then looking over it countless times and with prodding by many who read the book, I realized I wasn't done. So I decided to sit down and reflect on people I have met, both Irish and non-Irish, years of relentlessly chasing after a dream to obtain a doctorate degree in clinical psychology, new stories about my family with particular emphasis on my grandchildren, the return of cancer in 2002, and tumultuous times in 2003.

I am also writing this book in the hopes that my family will finally know just how much I appreciate each and every one of them and how grateful I am for their help and support. I am so sorry they had to jump on board that roller coaster ride in the summer of 2003, but the biggest lesson of that summer for all of us is realizing how blessed we are to be together.

How did the title of this book, _Please Call Me Sheila_, evolve? I was baptized "Julia," but the name never stuck. Everybody called me Sheila, except for when I was in the intensive care unit at St. Joseph's Hospital in 2003. There I was "Julia" until my daughters corrected them and a nurse put a sign over my bed, which read, "Please call me Sheila."

There seems to be some truth that names are interchangeable, as my friend Sean Radley claims. Sean, the curator of the Millstreet Museum, took me to places I had never been to or seen in my life when I visited Ireland in 2000. If you think about it, he's right. How often do you learn that Frank is Francis or Millie is

Millicent or Becky is Rebecca? Then there was Harry Truman. He did not have a middle name, so he stuck an "S" after his first name. I didn't have a middle name either, but I do now. Like Truman, I am proud to have an "S" after my first name.

I have been accused of picking up strays on my daily walks or strolls at shopping malls or coming out of church. My "strays" will get special mention in this book. I guess it is part of my nature to introduce myself with, "Hi, my name is Sheila, what's your name? "From there the ice is broken and friendships develop. For the purposes of this book, my "strays" will appear in the form of vignettes or sketches. I will lean on my family and friends to reminisce about past experiences and their own memories of things.

Finally, what should happen if the Irish banshee should take me across the great divide before completing this book? Since it took me 15-years to complete my first book, it's a valid concern. This time I hope to improve my speed. I have been very lucky, as my husband Jay does encourage me to keep a journal. Regardless, if I don't complete this book I can't help but remember that it didn't work out too badly for Franz Schubert who was famous for his Unfinished Symphony.

Irish Landscape, Millstreet, Descending Clara Mountain

THE DETROIT CONNECTION

BRIDGE OVER THE RIVER ROUGE

For 24-years we lived in a three-bedroom ranch with a finished basement and screened in porch on busy Telegraph Road in Detroit. Jay and I bought the house before we wed in May of 1957. After the service and the wedding brunch at the Park Sheldon Hotel in Detroit, we had a reception dinner with close friends and family in the finished basement of our new home. That dinner marked the beginning of two decades of happy memories.

For a long time, the Upper Rouge Stream separated our house from St. Eugene Church and school, as well as from Taft High School. The only way to cross the Rouge was to drive and take 7 Mile or 8 Mile Roads.

Thanks to Mrs. Hunsinger, our state representative who lived just west of Telegraph Road, funds were obtained to construct two walkover bridges. One bridge provided safe passage over busy Telegraph, and the other (more importantly for us) provided a way across the Rouge River between 7 and 8 Mile Roads.

After the bridge was built, there was no longer any need to carpool the kids in good weather. All they had to do was take Frisbee to Shiawassee, then walk over the new bridge. That's how the mighty Rouge was conquered, leaving everyone who lived on both sides of the stream with a pleasant walk. Thanks, Mrs. Hunsinger.

Dressed up for dinner at, Grand Hotel Mackinac Island

TOBOGGANING AT BONNIE BROOK

Bonnie Brook Golf Course would close down in the late fall and with the arrival of snow provide us a wonderful place to toboggan. We weren't supposed to do this on Bonnie Brook's property, so we tobogganed after dark and got away with it. I guess the owners were concerned with the liability factor.

Thanks to my husband's brother, Bud, and his wife Helen, we inherited a four-seat toboggan and shared it with other kids who lived in the neighborhood. Those challenging hills don't look at all challenging today. Yes, your mind and memories do work tricks in making things in the past appear so much larger.

It was on one of our outings that I met and made friends with the Murray's, fresh from Ireland and living in the recently built Bonnie Brook Apartments. As a matter of fact, they had just arrived and we helped them get settled in.

Fate is a funny thing. As much as we hated seeing the Bonnie Brook Apartments going up and considering how hard we fought its development by joining with our neighbors to hire an attorney to stop construction because of the congestion we knew it would cause, we never would have met the Murray's without them.

I first met Helen on the snowy slopes of Bonnie Brook with her children. Her husband Patrick and his brother Carl (married to Grace) are both doctors who came to America for additional training in their respective fields of rehabilitation and obstetrics.

Eventually the Murray's moved to the Bloomfield Hills area. Like us, they liked to entertain, and as no surprise, lots of Irish showed up at their doorstep, especially if they were doctors. It was a sad day for us when we learned that the Murray's were returning to Ireland. With their enhanced skills, they moved to Dublin where Carl was in charge of a maternity hospital and Patrick heads up the rehabilitation section of another large hospital.

Although we stayed friends and even slipped away from Millstreet on a trip back to Ireland in the 1990s to visit them in Dublin, we will always miss their company and close friendship.

What did Helen and Patrick miss most about America? Chocolate chips no less! So we brought over several bags, which are like gold in Ireland.

MARY & JOE

I had a wonderful neighbor, Mary McGrath, who lived on the street behind me in Detroit. I still remember jumping our fence to get to her house. We became fast friends during the early years of our marriages and remain best friends to this day.

Mary's parents were from Ireland and insisted that she marry only a man of Irish background. Joe fit the bill. He was an Irish Catholic who had dropped out of the seminary to pursue his interest in teaching, and specifically remedial reading. Very little was written about remedial reading at the time and Joe was actually a pioneer in the field, developing reading programs and opening his first clinic on Detroit's west side. This instant success led to the opening of other reading clinics.

THE FIRST TRIP BACK TO IRELAND

The girls and I went to Ireland in 1963 with Mary McGrath and her mother. While they toured around the country doing the bed and breakfast thing, we stayed at my childhood home in Millstreet where the children discovered a new world as they went from city life to a life in the country.

We were there for two weeks and it was the girl's first experience in farm living, and yes, they had ambivalent feelings about it. Sometimes they were happy and sometimes they were scared by the farm animals. It usually depended on who was doing the chasing. They had a great time running after the turkeys and the hens that would fly away when the girls tried to catch them. But it was a different story when the little piglets or the geese would come running after them.

The kales in my hometown consist of our family's 80-acres of pasture land. It was here where the girls spent a great deal of time playing with frogs that lived in the many small water streams down at the kales. For Meg and Kit living on the farm was unique since everyday promised to bring new experiences.

My family referred to the girls as "the little Yanks" and also informed me that I had lost my brogue. This was the first time Meg and Kit met their grandfather who had some difficulty understanding them in the beginning, but by the end of the second week their granddad had no more difficulty. He adored the children. Sadly, Mum had passed away earlier.

We missed the flight back to Detroit because we arrived late at the Shannon airport and our seats were sold. Poor Mary and her mother, they had made it to the airport in time and spent the whole flight across the Atlan tic worrying about us. But there was no need to worry. A Delta flight from Paris to Detroit was di verted to Shannon to pick us up along with four other passengers who also had the misfortune of

County Mayo house. Oct. 2004 Margaret O'Sullivan and Cathy

missing the original flight. It's still amazes me that the Delta flight arrived only 45-min utes after the charter flight landed.

Jay was waiting for us at Metro Airport when he heard his name called over the loud speaker. They asked him to report to the Delta desk where the trip coordinator told him what happened and not to worry. Later, he ran into Mary and her mother after their plane had landed. They were all concerned about Meg, Kit and I. After he explained what had happened, Mary told Jay this could only happen to Sheila. He agreed, telling me later that he never expected to be paged in an airport full of travelers.

THE DETROIT RIOTS

Mary and Joe had two daughters while they were still living in Detroit. With the success of the schools, they moved to the Whitmore Lake area, near Six Mile and Spencer Roads where they built a gorgeous home on approximately 80 acres of farmland. They had two more children after they moved there, a girl and a boy.

We visited Mary, Joe and the children regularly, but one visit stands out in particular. It was a Sunday afternoon in the summer of 1967. On the way home we heard on the radio there was rioting in Detroit. We made it home safely and stayed glued to the television set, watching the story unfold. There was some comfort in knowing that the neighbors on either side of us were Detroit policemen. One even offered us a pistol, which we refused, of course. Jay said he would probably shoot himself in the foot if he tried to use it.

The next day was Monday. The city shut down and people were told to stay home. On Tuesday, people were asked to report to work, if possible. Jay, along with a few others formed a carpool and ventured to work, driving down Grand River to downtown Detroit. At Clairmont and Grand River, they began to see evidence of the riot's destruction, broken glass and buildings looted and burned. But as Jay said, no one wanted to sight see, everyone wanted to keep moving as fast as possible. As I think back on it now, I wonder if my husband and his fellow bankers were brave, dedicated, stupid or perhaps a combination of all of the above.

BECKER'S ACRES

Mary and Joe's move to the country inspired us to look for some land of our own. We found the perfect spot in Salem Township and closed the deal in December 1969. We called our 10 acres "Becker's Acres" and we still own it today.

When we purchased Becker's Acres it was with the thought that we were going to build on it. Then Jay took a dry run to his work at the Renaissance Center in downtown Detroit. The drive would have given him an 84-mile commute so that was the end of that.

Even still, we didn't have to build a house and live on the farm for the girls to grow up there. We spent so much time there that in my opinion Becker's Acres really was the place where they were brought up.

PRIVATE SCHOOL

Meg and Kit attended parochial school at our church, St. Eugene, and then went onto Mercy High School. St Eugene was only one and a half miles from our home and I always drove them in bad weather. But when it was nice, they could walk through the fields at the back of our house and over the small bridge state representative Hunsinger had managed to get for us.

Meg and Kit were taught by nuns and they were excellent to my children. The nuns at St. Eugene's can't even be compared to the hor-

Pumpkin Party at Becker's Acres.

rible nuns I had to cope with back in Ireland. Here they were only interested in the student's welfare, educational outcome, and family concerns. We were so impressed with them that my husband and I even took math classes from one, very petite nun. She was a brain at trying to explain to us modern techniques and new math.

ST. EUGENE CLOSES

Kit was in grade 8 when St. Eugene's School closed in 1973. Declining attendance and overwhelming financial debt forced the school to close. When the financial situation failed to improve, the church closed its doors in 1989, after 35-years of service to the community. The Archdiocese of Detroit later turned the building over to a Korean Catholic group. Many of our parishioners were very angry at the Archdiocese for letting that happen.

The Korean Catholic Church kept it for a few years until they built a new church in the suburbs. The neighborhood had become dangerous and apparently several parishioners who attended the early prayer service at the Korean Church had been robbed and threatened with violence near and around the building.

Once a year parishioners from St. Eugene's meet for dinner. The event is organized by a wonderful couple, Donna and Marty Jason, along with Judy Stec.

I love these get-togethers. We have a great time reminiscing about the past and catching-up on what everyone is doing. Now even children and grandchildren, who never once attended a Mass at St. Eugene's, come with their parents and grandparents to the annual dinner. All are welcome.

HORSESHOE LAKE & JACK COMES BACK

Mary introduced us to the Kelley's on Horseshoe Lake, which is located in the town of Whitmore Lake and is not far at all from Becker's Acres. The Kelley's invited us to enjoy the lake whenever we wanted to, and while we loved our farmland, it was nice to run out to Horseshoe Lake for a swim.

Jack Schenk, daughter Cathy, me

In the "small world" department, Jack Schenk, who was the best man at our wed ding in 1957, moved out to Horseshoe Lake to be closer to his work in Ann Arbor. He rented a home right next to—and you guessed it right—the Kelley's! With Jack living on Horse shoe Lake we now had his permission, along with the Kelley's permission, to use the lake.

Even though Jack and his wife had no children he still took on the task of being a Boy Scout leader in Whitmore Lake. He worked hard at it and had the grand idea of contacting a canoe manufacturer to supply canoes for a trip all the way down the Huron River. The publicity would be good for the canoe manufacturer and big news for a small town like Whitmore Lake. The kids would be faced with strenuous adventure, rowing, camping out at night and portaging around dams. Jack and his Boy Scouts troop were excited, but excitement turned to frustration and disappointment when none of the parents volunteered to help. Obviously one adult could not do it alone and the project was scrapped.

Jack has remained a good friend to us to this day and is mentioned in some detail in my first book, **_My Dream From Ireland To America_**. He has traveled extensively throughout the United States and if the truth be told, his long list of jobs would be in the Guinness World Book of Records.

POEMS BY JACK SCHENK

THE ODD COUPLE
Seen them in movies
And on TV
Such an odd couple
Could be Jay and me
Jay vote's right
I vote left
He likes to garden
Which I detest
He likes to plan
To the last detail
I'll do the opposite
Without fail
He likes cleanliness
All nice and neat
I'll never be accused
Of being a cleaning freak
In the kitchen
Jay is supreme
Just give me some pie
With a little ice cream
Expert food shopper
Hey, it is on sale
Check those coupons
He gets in the mail
I never shop for food
Or check out a sale
If I ever told you I did
It would be a false tale
Jay holds his jobs
For a very long time
Lots of different jobs
Is a habit of mine

Jay stays in one place
Detroit and Birmingham all his life
Lives in a nice home
With Sheila his wife
I've traveled all over
Had many homes
I can't help it
Just a guy who roams
Jay and I grew up together
Went to Catholic Central High
And I'm only kidding
He is really a great guy
He will always be my friend
Hope he thinks it too
But this is just a poem
And dedicated to you

Jay, Sheila and Cathy at home

POEM FOR SHEILA

Raised on a farm where Shamrocks grow
And Leprechaun's live
In wee pots of gold
Came to America
A young pretty Nurse
She is the subject
Of this little verse
Met a guy named Jay
And married him too
Had two little girls
By the time they were thru
Her name was Sheila
The salt of the earth
But still harkens back
To the land of her birth
Remember Sheila's pies
Not always the best
Some even failed
To pass the hardness test
Kind and generous
Perhaps to a fault
Tells all her friends
Knows what life is all about
Has opinions of her own
And speaks her mind
If you don't believe it
Just meet her sometime
Maybe free advice
Or even a critique
Always means well
So it can be a treat
Sheila has true grit
And courage too
A very good friend
With a heart so true
Enjoy seeing the Beckers
Friends a very long time
Over the many years
Great friends of mine

BIRMINGHAM: 1981

After twenty-four years life in our friendly neighborhood in Detroit began to change. I remember one day the neighbor who lived behind us came over to ask us if we saw someone jump our fence. The wife had come home from shopping and found a man in her house and apparently he jumped the fence and ran through our yard. Well that did it for Jay and we began house hunting.

The first real estate agent stopped talking to us when he found out how much we were willing to spend. But eventually found someone willing to work with us and in February of 1981 we moved into a corner ranch home on a quite little street in Birmingham.

Jay was able to take the SMART shuttle bus to the train station in Birmingham. From there he could take the train downtown to the Renaissance Center where he worked at Manufacturers National Bank. This worked well for him for two or three years until they stopped the commuter trains. So, several of the passengers got together at a meeting here at our house. They started their own vanpool and together rented a van through a company that promoted car-pooling. Three passengers, including Jay, took turns driving the Dodge Ram 15-passenger van, picking up the other riders and taking them downtown to work everyday.

Jay used the van service until he retired in 1989. The day after he retired, he took a lawn chair, table, and pitcher of lemonade along with the newspaper down to the end of our street. When the van came down the street it screeched to a stop at the sight of Jay. It was with great pleasure that he waived to his former commuter colleagues and toasted them good luck while relaxing comfortably with a newspaper and a cool glass of lemonade from his lawn chair at the end of our street. They had a great laugh as they waived back. Ironically, after that display of a life of leisure, Jay now says there aren't enough hours in the day for him to do all the things he wants to do.

MARY MOVES ON

Dark clouds eventually developed for our dear friends Mary and Joe. What happened to Joe's once successful business? Financial problems mixed with overwhelming tax liens soon led to bankruptcy. Was it because one of his partners left to become a competitor? Was it because his money was tied up in fixed assets that drained working capital? Joe always wanted to own and never lease. In the end, the empire collapsed and so did the marriage. Divorce was inevitable.

Mary is and always will be a survivor. Following the divorce, Mary relied on welfare assistance. Determined to get her life in order, she went into training and became a lab technician. Her life turned around when she obtained her degree and started working full time at the University of Michigan Hospital, giving her a way to support herself and her family. Then she married Jerry.

San Francisco, May 2004. Home of Tim and Ngoc Villalobos.

Jerry was a lifelong friend of Mary's who had previously been married but had lost his wife to a serious illness about 10-years earlier. He served in the military and was an active member of the Knights of Columbus and various Irish groups. We knew of Jerry too, but only casually, and we'll always regret that we didn't know him better.

THE WINGS OF A DOVE

Jerry fought a brave battle against cancer, but lost the war in March 2004. He spent his last days in hospice care.

To say it simply, Jerry was just a wonderful guy in every way. That his life touched us and so many others is undeniable. His unique, well-planned and well-attended funeral was a testament to how much he was loved.

Held at a funeral home located on the outskirts of the small town of Hamburg, between Brighton and Ann Arbor, Jerry's wake included the newly created luminous mysteries. For those not familiar with the rosary, there are four mysteries to meditate on: Joyful, Sorrowful, Glorious and Luminous. These mysteries reflect on biblical events concerning the life of Jesus. Each mystery consists of five reflections, or bible stories, for the faithful to meditate on as they recite ten Hail Mary's after each reflection. The Luminous mysteries tell the stories of the Baptism in the Jordan, the Wedding at Cana, the Proclamation of the Kingdom (Jesus' preaching), the Transfiguration, and the Institution of the Eucharist. Each mystery precedes the reciting of ten Hail Mary's for a total of 50 Hail Mary's.

After the rosary, a video of still shots was shown of Jerry's life, from his childhood to his military career, to his life with Mary. There were other mementos and photos on display as well. The Mass itself ended with a three gun military salute in the church parking lot, and what followed was absolutely memorable.

The grandchildren gathered together and formed a ring around a small wooden box that contained a white dove. The top of the box was removed and out flew a white dove that headed skyward, circling overhead until it disappeared out of view.

What wonderful symbolism. The release of the dove visually demonstrated the release of the soul to heaven. It was a beautiful conclusion and a touching tribute to a man so well liked.

Meanwhile, my dear Mary continues to be a survivor. And she will always remain so.

A MUSICAL RENAISSANCE

The music of Johan Sebastian Bach would perhaps be lost today had it not been for a friend of Felix Mendelssohn's, who brought some of Bach's musical scores to Mendelssohn's attention. Mendelssohn, a musical giant in his day, immediately recognized Bach's genius and made it his mission to find all of Bach's manuscripts. By doing so, he preserved Bach's music for the entire world to enjoy today.

Shrine of the Little Flower Church, Royal Oak concert. 2002

In a similar way, Dutch organist Willem Zwart, on a concert tour in California in the mid-1980's, was introduced to the music of my father-in-law, Professor René L. Becker. Zwart was given a score of Becker's First Organ Sonata in g minor by someone who attended the concert, which he took back with him to Holland. He mastered the score and recorded the music on LP in 1986, and later on CD in 1991.

The music became popular in Europe, but the lingering question was "who is Professor René Becker? "All they knew was that he was born in 1882 and died in 1956.

In the late 1990s, Jay and Gene Scott began pouring over musical scores and various bits of memorabilia concerning Jay's father, René Becker. Scott, a retired public relations writer and educator, is a lifelong friend of Jay who had written his masters dissertation at the University of Detroit on Professor Becker years earlier.

With Jay's help, Scott wrote a biographical article based on the new research and sent it to the publishers of *The American Organist* who immediately accepted the article and ran it in the November 2000 issue. *The American Organist* has been published for over 100-years and this wasn't the first time René Becker's name appeared on its pages. An article in 1918, predicted a bright future for the young composer.

Soon after The American Organist came out, the Dutch publication, *de Orgelvriend* (which means "friend of the organ"), contacted us to obtain permission to translate Scott's story for their magazine. As a result of these two articles, we learned that Everhard Zwart, Willem Zwart's son, had recorded Becker's sonata in Parris in 1999. Luckily, we were able to obtain a couple dozen copies of the recording and we shared them with family, friends and musical contacts.

Through correspondence with Everhard Zwart, we learned about his good friend and countryman, Johannes (John) Witte, who now lives in the Grand Rapids-Holland area of Michigan. Many people of Dutch background settled in this area, well known for its annual Tulip Festival.

Witte operated a very successful travel agency that booked choral groups to and from Europe. It was he who arranged for Everhard Zwart along with a choral group to appear in Grand Rapids in September 2001. By that time, we had sent many musical scores to Everhard and had formed a warm relationship with him and his family. Quite naturally we were determined to meet him in person and John Witte said he would make sure that Everhard would play some of René Becker's music.

Well, with the events of September 11th, the group came close to canceling its concert tour, but persistence prevailed. The choral group performed magnificently to a standing room audience and for us it was a magical moment when John Witte announced that my husband and I, as well as our children and grandchildren, were in the audience to hear the music of Professor René Becker. Witte had us stand and we were given a rousing ovation.

We tried to book Everhard at Detroit's Cathedral of the Most Blessed Sacrament for an all Becker concert played on the same Casavant organ Becker had played during his 13-year tenure at the cathedral. Unfortunately, the cathedral was in the midst of a 20-million dollar plus renovation and was entirely shut down. It was a big disappointment to Ever hard and to us. Our own parish, Holy Name in Birmingham, was also shut down for major renovation, but we managed to provide a venue for him in Royal Oak at the historic National Shrine of the Little Flower in the fall of 2002.

Family gathered following organ concert. San Francisco, May 2004

He played various selections, including Becker's First Organ Sonata.

Back in Holland, Everhard came out with his first DVD in 2003, which included Becker's Toccata in D. Everhard has played all three of Becker's Organ Sonatas in concert here in Michigan, Florida and California, as well as Toccata in D and choral works. My husband says the music is very difficult to play and requires the skill of a fully trained organist. Jay's father would certainly give Everhard's performance a nod of approval.

In March 2004, Everhard gave a series of concerts in Florida. The following May, he performed live in the San Francisco-Oakland area. Jay and I flew out to California with our daughter Meg to visit

Meg and I, Clearwater Beach, "pier 60" Mar. 2005

my brother Pat and his wife, Eileen. While we were there we took in the organ recital at the Cathedral of St. Mary of the Assumption in San Francisco. Today, the Becker's and the Zwart's are one big happy family.

PIPEDREAMS

Margaret O'Sullivan and her dad
Pat Millstreet. Ireland, Oct. 2004

Meanwhile, Meg sent a copy of Everhard's 1999 Paris recording of the First Organ Sonata in g minor to Michael Barone. Barone hosts a program called *Pipedreams* that is distributed to various National Public Radio Sta tions throughout the United States. Meg sent the recording in hopes that he would play Everhard's rendition of the Becker sonata on the air.

Barone had just moved into a house in St. Paul, Minnesota, and ironically the previous owner gave him a number of musical scores including the second and third organ sonatas of Profes sor René Becker. Barone's research into Becker's life did not uncover much so he put the scores aside. When he received the Paris record ing from Meg, along with the article from ___The American Organist___, it was an eye opener for him. Barone said yes, he would include the First Sonata in one of his programs and that "yes" turned into reality in September 2004, when Becker's music became part of a show entitled "American Sonatas."

It was an interesting program mix. Barone included music by an American-born musician trained in Germany (Buck), and a German-born musician who emigrated for a time to the United States (Hindemith), an American-born musician who lived in Germany (Sanders), an all-American musician who trained and lived in the United States (Larsen), and an Alsacian-born composer with German and French ties who spent the majority of his life in the US (Becker). Barone saved the best for last, ending the national broadcast with Everhard Zwart's recording of the First Organ Sonata much to the delight of everyone. It was truly a musical renaissance.

NEVER TOO LATE TO LEARN

Music in this family has always been very important, even for me, and I wasn't brought up in a musical family. As I sit down to play for my own amusement, I remember how I took full advantage of piano lessons when the opportunity presented itself. I was a student nurse in England when I made arrangements with the daughter of a patient who was a piano teacher. We agreed that I would take care of her dad on a weekly basis if she, in turn, would give me music lessons.

I bought a piano froma Red Cross nurse and put it in the living room of the nurse's home so I could practice daily. One day a supervisor said to me, "Sheila, was that you playing? "I felt very proud because I knew I was progressing.

Cathy, Meg in Ireland, Oct 2004

NO JOBS IN IRELAND

I really never wanted to leave Ireland, but back then jobs were scarce and colleges were expensive. Today, Ireland enjoys a high employment rate and colleges and universities are free and available to everyone. But in 1955, jobs in Ireland were virtually non-existent and there was no such thing as a free education. The economy was poor and there was a surplus of registered nurses for the few hospital positions that were available.

In England, I read in my student magazine that Grace Hospital here in Michigan was hiring nurses. So I applied and was accepted.

I arrived in Michigan in January of 1955, and worked as a graduate nurse for six months until I was able to sit the state boards and become a registered nurse.

What a shock for me when I started at Grace Hospital in the obstetrics department. I had participated in or delivered about 400 babies in England where I was a State Certified Midwife, but here, I wasn't allowed to deliver a single baby. All I did was pass instruments to the doctors. Bored, I finally asked to be transferred into a medical-surgical unit. I stayed there until I married Jay in 1957.

WAYNE STATE UNIVERSITY: 1955–1957

I started college part time at Wayne State University after only a few months in this country. It was here that I met our life-long friend Tony Bersani in a

Margaret O'Sullivan, Theresa Kelleher at Jerry nad Jenny's wedding, County Mayo

class. He was a friendly student in my class who spoke to me frequently. One day, I introduced him to a girl-friend of mine outside of class. I said, "Tony, this is Joan and I have class now. "Tony's parents were not overjoyed when I first introduced them. They had an Italian girl picked out for him. But despite his parent's initial objection, Tony and Joan eventually married and became the proud parents of two boys and a girl.

When I started at Wayne State I was hoping to eventually go to medical school, but then I met my wonderful husband, Jay, and my plans changed. We were married on May 4, 1957. Margaret Mary was born on June 4, 1958 and Catherine Angela came to us almost two years later, on March 22,1960. I was lucky to be able to stay home with them, and believe me, I enjoyed every moment. I remember dancing with Meg when she was a baby to the music of Rachmaninoff until we finally wore out the recording. Jay was not happy with me, as he could not replace that record.

I returned to Wayne State briefly when Meg was a student there in 1977, just before I enrolled at the University of Detroit. Meg was in one of my classes, and like all kids, she didn't want anyone to know we were related so we never sat together. On the last day of class the professor said "Oh it looks like I have two Becker's in this class. "Meg wore a big smile that day and later graduated with a degree in psychology and a minor in accounting. The accounting degree is what she is using at the present, but I have no doubt that the psychology degree plays a strong role in her work.

UNIVERSITY OF DETROIT: 1977–1982

When the girls were both in college I decided to return to my studies, only this time I went to the University of Detroit because all registered nurses received sixty-four credit hours to start. I took just one class per semester and was the oldest student in my day classes. The students attending evening classes were closer to my own age and we had much more in common, but the young classmates during the day were wonderful to me and treated me just like their own Mom.

I loved the University of Detroit. The professors were so helpful, especially Professor Tobias who was instrumental in helping me to write my thesis which was related to families coping with substance abuse. Jesuit teaching is considered among the very best and is usually expensive, but I have always said that one cannot equate education with dollars and cents.

I was at University of Detroit from 1977-1982. I received a Bachelor of Social Work and a Bachelor of Arts, as well as a Masters in Guidance and Counseling. In 1982, I left the didactic University of Detroit for a totally different experience at the Center for Humanistic Studies.

CENTER FOR HUMANISTIC STUDIES: 1982 TO 1989–THE RISING PHOENIX

I was working as a psychiatric nurse at Providence Hospital where I was frustrated with issues on the unit. A social worker that was attending the Center for Humanistic Studies encouraged me to take a look at the school. When I did, I discovered a unique graduate school and research center that was dedicated to the art and science of being human. At this school the em phasis was on teaching and I, the learner, was central to their teaching. And so my journey began. The education I received at CHS was life changing and permeated not just my professional, but my personal life as well.

This was the best experience of my life. CHS taught me to look inside myself first. I learned that I would need to make some internal changes before I would be capable of helping others. "Trust the process and be authentic," that was their motto, and it really was the best thing for me. Instead of always being analytical, I learned to get out of my head and get into my own gut feelings.

The teachers were just wonderful to me. They accepted me and treated me like a special human being. There, I learned how to "trust the process" which

May. 2004. Back yard with Pat & Eily with family and Everhard Zwart. San Francisco.

meant working with the future and knowing that it was my choice to look at the future in either a negative or positive way.

Learning to "trust the process" increased my self-esteem. Weekly group therapy sessions helped. It was there that I was able to express my true feelings, which weren't always accepted by my colleagues and that made for some very tense moments. Some of my fellow students criticized me because they didn't think my facial expressions changed to the extent that they thought they should. I wasn't "emotional" enough for them. But that was because I had great control, and I always have, and soon I began to ignore their criticism and "trust the process" and that helped to increase my confidence and self-esteem.

THE CENTER FOR HUMANISTIC STUDIES: A BRIEF HISTORY

The history of the Center for Humanistic Studies begins with the Merrill-Palmer Institute, which is located on historic East Ferry Street in Detroit. East Ferry is on the north end of Detroit's Cultural Center, just a few short blocks from Wayne State University. It was here, that in 1919, the newly formed Institute acquired the shingle-style mansion of famed industrialist and Asian art collector, Charles Lang Freer. His name may sound familiar. His art collection, which used to be right here in Detroit, is at the Freer Gallery in the Smithsonian Institute in Washington, DC instead of Detroit because the Detroit Institute of Arts reportedly refused it. Another lost treasure for the city.

As the Merrill-Palmer Institute grew, they purchased several more stately homes on East Ferry Street. Many of these homes were converted into dorms. One of them, Detroit's first all-cement home was built by real estate developer Henry G. Stevens in 1913. The Merrill-Palmer Institute bought it in 1942, and 38-years later the classic revival mansion became the Center for Humanistic Studies.

Thanks to our old friend, Gene Scott, I can recount a bit more of East Ferry history here. Gene's book, ***Detroit Beginnings: Early Villages and Old***

Neighborhoods, contains a brief, but informative description of the East Ferry neighborhood.

"*A registered State and national historic district, this is the first three blocks of East Ferry east of Woodward to Beaubien. It is another fashionable residential area that was developed in the late 19th century. The larger homes are closer to Woodward and include the Col. Frank Hecker house, now offices of a law firm. East Ferry was home for some of the cities corporate leaders, such as Charles Freer of the Peninsular Car Company and William Jackson of Michigan State Telephone. It became predominantly Jewish after 1920, and later African American. Still on East Ferry is the association of woman's clubs, the Omega Psi Phi black fraternity, Your Heritage House Museum, and the Fritz Funeral home, which was the residence of the nationally known Prophet Jones. Four homes were recently restored as a 42-room hotel, The Inn on Ferry Street. The Inn received the Detroit Historical District Advisory Commissions Triumph Award for this historic preservation project. The street is named after Dexter Ferry, the seed company magnet who had a large seed farm in this area. He himself never lived here. It is noted that the seed company, after many years in Detroit, moved to San Francisco and is now know as the Ferry-Morse seed company.* "Sound familiar?

For years, the Merrill-Palmer Institute was considered a quality school of higher learning. Despite its reputation, the Institute ran into financial problems and was bankrupt by 1980. Wayne State University would eventually take over, but not before two of the most respected professors, Clark Moustakas and Cereta Perry, took on the ambitious task of forming a new, independent school to carry on the reputation of the Merrill-Palmer Institute. They acquired the Henry G. Stevens home from the Merrill-Palmer Institute in a lawsuit, and in 1980, the Center for Humanistic Studies was born.

STUDENT LIFE

There were 22 students in my class when I started in 1982, but only 17 completed the program. One of the students who dropped out was a young registered nurse whose sister, a resident medical doctor, took her own life as the pressure of school was too much for her. My classmate did not want what happened to her sister to happen to her, and whilst I did sympathize with her, I really felt her loss from our group.

My fellow students and I occasionally socialized outside the classroom and we were fortunate to have a student whose family owned a yacht with live-in caretakers who handled all the entertaining. One day this student invited the entire class on a cruise. Well that year the water level was very low on Lake St. Clair and in the channels leading to the Lake. We got stuck and that caused the boat to shake a great deal. Items began to fall from shelves and I was concerned for one of our classmates who was pregnant at the time. Finally, the coast guard came and towed us back in, with no further problems. Despite the scary moments out in the Lake, we all had a delightful lunch and really enjoyed the rest of day.

INTERNSHIPS

At the Center for Humanistic Studies students had a variety of internships to complete for graduation. My favorite one was at a place called Gateway, a community mental health facility. Gateway clients had no insurance and no money.

I developed a good rapport with my clients and as a result I had very few cancellations. It was at our weekly supervisory meetings with a fully licensed psychologist that I learned many of my own colleagues had to fill out forms for no-show patients. My patients must have really liked me because I never had to do this.

A few years later, in 1990, Gateway helped me organize the 10th anniversary party for CHS. I put together a dinner dance at the Birmingham Community House. Gateway let me use their facility for stuffing envelopes to send out invitations. This was a black tie affair, and over 100 people attended. Proceeds from the dinner dance raised $1200 for CHS.

PLAY THERAPY

Clark Moustakas was an early pioneer of play therapy and so play therapy was an important part of a CHS education. I participated in play therapy with a family who lived several blocks away from the school. They had three or four children and I used to drive them to our sessions so the mother wouldn't have to spend money on a taxi since it was too dangerous for her to walk. That wasn't the only thing I did for them. I always made a big fuss about their birthdays, bringing in a small cake so the family could join me in holding hands and singing "Happy Birthday" together.

The play therapy room was in the basement. It was filled with a variety of toys and games and I would allow each child to pick their favorite to play with. I learned a great deal from these children, I guess you could say that I learned as much from our sessions as they did. It was here where they could verbalize their feelings regarding their home, family, neighborhood, school and friends. In play therapy they showed me how their mother killed rats in their apartment, how the landlord refused to fix anything and how they were jealous of the attention their mother gave other siblings.

When I drove them home after our sessions there was a man hanging outside their apartment who would try to sell me cocaine. Here they lived in a neighborhood that was rampant with illegal substance abuse, but they weren't part of it.

In the play therapy room in the basement at CHS, I learned how lucky my own children have been all their lives. Their living conditions were not at all like the way these children had to live. It was here that I really began to appreciate everything Jay and I had been able to give them.

MY DISSERTATION

I may have forgotten the exact date, but there is one particular day in 1987 that I will never forget. On this day, Dr. Clark Moustakas announced to our class that each student should "pick out your own dissertation. "He said it should be about something you would like to change.

At that time I was working in a psychiatric hospital and saw many things I would like to change. I was stressed out with hospital policy, and I thought about how I could help the hospital make some positive changes. That's how I picked my topic "*The Experience of Psychiatric Nurses Coping with Stress in the Workplace.*" This study came from a desire to understand how individual psychiatric nurses in a psych unit cope with stress and a belief that this understanding might contribute to the available knowledge of the work psychiatric nurses do to help develop ways to alleviate burnout, turnover, depression and other detrimental outcomes due to stress that often deprive the profession of its most talented members.

I interviewed ten registered nurses for a period of three to four months, analyzed a mountain of literature at four different universities, studied psychiatric nurses in India and reviewed endless amounts of pre-existing data.

I can't tell you how many times I received my dissertation chapters back from my great professor, Dr. Cereta Perry. I finally finished it though, and that was only because of the patience of the staff. The University of Michigan Press printed "*The Experience of Psychiatric Nurses Coping with Stress in the Workplace*" and I have since offered it to both the University of Detroit and Oakland University.

I completed my studies in 1989, and graduated with a Psychology Specialist Degree. In the end, I spent about $50,000 to $60,000 on my education. But no matter how long I studied and no matter how much money I spent, the longer I went the more I realized how little I knew.

THE MOVE TO FARMINGTON HILLS: 2002

The Stevens' mansion on East Ferry Street was more than adequate for the Center of Humanistic Studies in the beginning, but there was limited parking. Like so many of my fellow students, I took advantage of the parking structure at the Park Sheldon Hotel. It was a block away from the school and, incidentally, the place where Jay and I had our wedding brunch in 1957. But nothing ever stays the same. The Park Sheldon Hotel was converted into retirement apartments, which later turned into condos. The mansion was sold to a law firm in 2003 and CHS moved to a new facility in Farmington Hills.

The new campus is located right next to Oakland Community College. I

Theresa, Pat, Eileen and Paddy at Jerry's, wedding. Oct. 2004

attended the dedication ceremony in September 2002, but the old mansion on East Ferry Street and the Park Sheldon Hotel held happy memories for me and I had ambivalent feelings about the relocation. But everything must grow and progress in its own unique way and it was time for me to "trust the process" and move on to discover what the future had in store for the school.

Despite my personal feelings, September 21, 2002 was a miraculous, magical day for CHS. For many, many, months, planning committee members met, designed, and imagined all sorts of ways to blend the significance of the move into this moment in time. In fact, the committee also plotted and schemed behind closed doors to keep the ceremony details a secret surprise. As each detail was checked off and the schedule drew closer, there was a feverish pitch of excitement at the Center.

On the eve of the big day, torrential rains flooded the new campus. CHS president, Kerry Moustakas, (who happens to be the daughter of co-founder, Clark Moustakas) received phone calls with vivid descriptions of acres of mud.

Builder, David Dowling, was called in to assess the situation. Dowling devised a rescue mission. He ordered truckloads of gravel and dirt to create a dry area for guests attending the ceremony under the tent.

CHS was in luck. By 3 PM, the day turned magnificent and sunny. Over 100 alumni, students, faculty, staff, neighbors and friends attended the building dedication at 26811 Orchard Lake Road in Farmington Hills. It was with awe that I stood before the building that would become our new home.

Later, more than 150 people from as far away as Virginia, Massachusetts, Washington, D. C. and California gathered at the Birmingham Temple for a 5 PM reception. We all listened as the founders recounted stories of how CHS was born from the Merrill-Palmer Institute. In her speech, President Kerry Moustakas called CHS "a place where historical roots spread wings to create the future."

After the presentations, there was a fabulous strolling dinner at the Birmingham Temple where the entire CHS community had a chance to informally meet and greet one another. It was a chance to meet new people and to catch-up with members from my own class, the class of 1989. The program that was distributed at dinner included an article on "Scholarly Projects" produced by the faculty, alumni and students. It was here that my own published book, ___My Dream from Ireland to America___, was included under the Alumni heading.

When the Center for Humanistic Studies began in 1980, they offered both Master of Arts and Psychology Specialist degree programs. The ensuing years brought new programs, more courses, a doctorial program, additional faculty, and better technology. Much has transpired in the last 25-years, but one element remains unchanged, and that is the impact and influence that CHS has had on me.

Each of us is a part of the CHS legacy. We each possess threads of its teachings, and when we join our hands and hearts we create a distinctive and exquisite tapestry, rich in color and texture. We are like-minded individuals of today who are needed to enhance the vision of yesterday. This is only done by becoming an active participant in the life of CHS.

PhD STUDIES: 1989–1994

Before the Center of Humanistic Studies had developed its own PhD program, they were affiliated with the Union Institute & University in Cincinnati, Ohio. The Union Institute is an alternative school of higher learning designed to offer smaller schools a doctoral program. Here students who are mostly working professionals can design their own PhD program, chair and select their own doctoral committee, and study from a distance either online or through affiliated schools such as CHS. The curriculum requires students to participate in ten "peer days" which are locally held educational programs. I hosted two "peer days" during my time at the Union Institute. The program also requires students to attend seminars that are held at different locations around the country.

I learned about the Union Institute and University at a Colloquium held at the St. Mary's Conference Center in Monroe. Dr. Clark Moustakas, Dr. Perry and other members of the CHS faculty provided an enormous amount of information on the program which left me feeling anxious and overwhelmed and convinced the whole project was beyond my grasp until Dr. Perry pulled a group of us aside to a corner of the room and had us join her in this place of clarity. I suddenly realized that I was capable of doing it. A great weight was lifted from my shoulders. Knowing that I had the help of Dr. Perry and my dissertation committee to guide me helped me to develop the positive attitude I needed to push forward.

I completed two doctoral level internships in psychology that I planned and developed with my doctoral committee to integrate theory, research and practice. These internships totaled 2000 hours of supervised psychological studies, activities and services that fulfilled state requirements and provided me with a variety of experiences and challenges in clinical psychological.

I had other internships to do as I pursued my PhD. I did 1000 hours at a walk in clinic where I was exposed to all kinds of problems and developed a great rapport with my patients who said that I really "told it like it is. "I did another internship at Dr. Lucas' outpatient nutritional clinic at Beaumont hospital where the majority of the patients were on a special liquid diet to lose weight. And I completed another 500 hours in the Geriatric unit of Botsford Hospital in 1990, where I learned a great deal about psychiatric testing.

It was during my internship at Botsford Hospital that I learned I had ovarian cancer. I remember that I was sitting in my office with my supervisor when my doctor called and advised me to see an oncologist without telling me why. He didn't have to tell me, I knew that a referral to an oncologist meant only one thing, cancer.

I was lucky. The cancer was encapsulated, which meant that it was only in one area and had not spread. Botsford Hospital was wonderful and gave me as much time as I needed to recover so I took off for a few months until my strength returned.

During this scary time I found that attending Union Institute seminars provided unique learning opportunities on significant topics that helped me deal with my illness. My seminar on dreams in particular taught me to focus on positive dreams to cope with my own cancer.

I received my doctorate from the Union Institute & University at the Center for Humanistic Studies on September 24, 1994. I look back on my graduation from the Union Institute & University with a smile. I can see myself, as I received my diploma, saying "I made it, I made it. "And I can hear all the clapping as I danced off the stage singing again and again "I made it! I made it!"

The words for me were probably more significant than anyone else realized. I didn't just make it through my PhD program, I made it through cancer. There were moments when I wasn't sure I would ever walk across that stage to get my diploma. From my perspective I had really, really made it in more ways than one.

MY TRAVELS

THREE GENERATIONS RETURN TO IRELAND, 1999

In 1999, six of us, representing three generations, went to Ireland on a family trip. Meg made all the arrangements before we arrived and we had a great time. She should have been a travel agent.

We stayed at the beautiful five-star Hotel Europe on the outskirts of Killarney. The hotel, equipped with every available comfort, sits on acres of mag

Holocaust Cantata concert, at the Holocaust Center, Farmington Hills, Michigan

nificently groomed land that include a golf course and horseback riding stables. The Hotel Europe is owned and staffed by Germans and hearing so many European accents made me feel like we were at a hotel on the Continent.

I grew up in Ireland but until I actually stayed there I'd never even heard of the Hotel Europe. I'd wondered all over that area when I was a child but I had no memory of even seeing the building before. What's even more ironic is that the wife of an ex-boyfriend of mine from Michigan had once worked as the hotel photographer. What a small world it is.

The Hotel Europe was our headquarters in Ireland. We invited all of our relatives to visit us there so we wouldn't have to drive. Driving on the opposite side of the street on narrow, winding Irish roads is very dangerous. I should know. I got into an accident in Millstreet when I drove too close to a parked car. When I got out of my car to look for the owner, the neighbors said, "Oh, he is in that bar".

I went in and he came out to look at the damage. When I tried to give him my license he said "Go away, as you have done more damage to your car than to mine". That was the last day I drove in Ireland.

The only driving exception we made was to visit my sister Nora. She and her family lived in Killarney and Nora was going through radiation treatment for breast cancer. I had a feeling I would not see her again. Unfortunately I was right. Nora passed away six months later.

THE "GIANT, DEMON, IRISH FLY" BY JULIE WASHABAUGH

My grandchild wrote the following essay as a school project. It's a wonderful story from our trip to Ireland.

"I never knew how afraid I was of flies until I went to Ireland.

One morning my family and I were at a fancy restaurant in Ireland. There were people from all over the world there (including us). It was a warm, sunny, summer day outside so many of the windows were open. Unfortunately a giant fly realized this and flew into the building and landed on my glass. It was the biggest fly I had ever seen. Scared and amazed by its size, I dropped my fork. It made a loud clanking noise that echoed throughout the entire restaurant. My Mom quietly scolded me saying, 'Julie we are in a very nice restaurant, don't make so much noise.

A few minutes went by, and then the fly came back. But this time it landed on my Aunt Meg's hair. She jumped up and started screaming. My mom was also screaming and ran over and tried to get the giant fly out. Meanwhile Meg is jumping up and down screaming. "Get it out! Get it out! It is sucking out my brains!"

Realizing that it was not coming out, my mom grabbed the newspaper and began hitting her on the head with it. All this time, my sister and I were slouching down in our seats hoping that no one would see us. But everyone had their eyes on my mom and my aunt jumping up and down, screaming at

Hotel Europe, Killarney, Ireland. Jay and Daughter Meg

the top of their lungs, and my mom hitting her sister with a newspaper. Finally the fly got out. The two of them, cheeks reddened, sat down. A few people in the back of the room clapped, and I said in a quiet voice, 'and you yelled at me for dropping my fork? 'Later we realized it was all because Meg used the Hotel's mint-candy scented shampoo."

DENY'S FUNERAL: MARCH 2001

I returned to Ireland for my brother's funeral in 2001, but I didn't realize at the time that that was why I was going. My brother had been very ill and I wanted to see him so I booked the trip, got on the plane and headed back to my childhood home.

Jay got the telephone call that Deny had passed away soon after the plane took off. That was quite an experience for me, to step off the airplane and learn my brother had died. But that was only the beginning.

I was met at Shannon Airport by my nephew's wife. She drove me to the university where my nephew is a teacher. Then he drove me to Millstreet where my brother's body was in the morgue. What a shock that was. I had no idea that the morgue was the funeral home and that going to the morgue was considered routine in Ireland. It was here, in the morgue that the rosary was read.

The next day Deny's remains were taken to Millstreet Church and he was buried from there. I could not believe how people stood by his coffin in the parking lot, shaking hands with the family after the funeral mass.

I wasn't comfortable with that so I went straight to the car, only to discover that I'd been followed by my schoolmates. Despite the occasion, it was great to see all of them again.

FUNERAL LUNCH

The funeral lunch was held in a bar across from my brother-in-laws house where I was staying. At the luncheon, I sat with my old neighbor, Mrs. O'Sullivan, and her daughter who now has children of her own. When I was growing up, it was in this lady's home that I was introduced to Ketchup, cookies, and cake.

I went to visit Mrs. O'Sullivan before returning back to the USA. My brother-in-laws house was about 45 minutes away from Mrs. O'Sullivan's, and from her house is just another short fiveminute walk to my childhood home. I wanted to walk to both places, but my sister Theresa, who took care of Deny for years, didn't want me to go and insisted on driving me. Theresa was worried about me and didn't understand how much I really loved walking.

FLORIDA KEYS: A CHANGE OF PATTERNS.

Having traveled overseas many times, especially to Ireland, my husband and I began to wonder "why are we doing this? "Spending long hours in a plane is now much more than we can tolerate. Like the time we went to Hong Kong to see Jay's brother-in-law, Joe Smith and his wife Vern, and our great friends, Shafi and Lillian. We went through thirteen time zones and spent nine teen hours traveling. So to our relatives in

Norma and Bill Washabaugh with our family outside Keys residence.

Ireland, England, France and the U. S. A., our message is simple: It's your turn! My brother Pat and his wife Eileen got the message, they came from San Francisco to visit us twice in less than a year, and that is a five-hour journey.

Florida is the one exception we still make. We traditionally go down to Clearwater Beach for a couple weeks of sunshine and spectacular sunsets in March. Jay's brother had a home down there when he passed away in the 1970s, but Jay didn't want to buy it. One week in Florida and he's anxious to come home. I could stay there forever. I love walking on the beach in the early morning, enjoying the lovely view of the ocean

Family gathered behind Big Pine Keys residence.

and watching the seagulls as they fly close to shore hoping for a gift of food from a generous sunbather.

As I walk along the beach, I frequently dream of walking on that famous beach, Inch, in County Kerry.

We added a second Florida vacation in 2002. That year we had the opportunity to go down to the Florida Keys for Christmas, and it was an opportunity we couldn't resist.

Our son-in-law Tom's parents, Bill and Norma, bought a stately mansion on Big Pine Key, which is 31 miles north of Key West. Up until a few years ago, Bill and Norma traveled down to Florida in an R/V, trading up to a bigger and better one every so often. The place they always took the RV to in the Keys was eventually sold and after some convincing by their family, Bill and Norma went house hunting. That's when they came across a place to die for and made a wise investment. Purchasing this home made financial sense, since they traded a depreciating asset, like the R/V for a simply gorgeous house that is gaining in value by leaps and bounds everyday.

Bill and Norma now spend four months out of each year in the Keys, while different family members take turns vacationing there throughout the rest of the year. For us it meant trading Christmas trees for palm trees.

On this, our first Christmas Day departure to Florida, we booked our flight to Miami and rented an SUV for all seven of us to make the long trek to Big Pine Key. Bad move. It takes three hours to get to Big Pine or as long as it takes to travel from Detroit to Miami. And to make matters worse, nothing much is open on Christmas, so when you do find an open store you can expect to pay top dollar for basic necessities, like a quart of milk for $3. The following year we were much smarter and booked a connector flight to Key West, where it was a snap to rent an SUV and travel the short distance to Big Pine Key.

THE HOUSE ON THE KEYS

The home, with maid's quarters, is located at the end of a canal leading to the Gulf of Mexico. To the east is U. S. Highway 1 and just beyond it lies the Atlantic Ocean.

The house was built by a young couple who received a large financial settlement in a lawsuit against General Motors. Despite the settlement, they could not maintain the house and they put it up for sale at over a million dollars. Bill and Norma added an elevator, remodeled the kitchen and landscaped the grounds. Today, it is worth over 2 million dollars.

There are four rooms upstairs, one of which is used as a computer room which I love. Downstairs there is a master suite. Outside, the maids' quarters, which can be used as a guesthouse, has its own suite with a bathroom. Meg told Tom's father that she'd be willing to be the maid anytime so she could take advantage of all the wonderful things the area has to offer. There are hiking trails, a tennis court, parks and beaches for snorkeling and swimming.

Big Pine Key Washabaugh residence.

Bill and Norma have a full time gardener who maintains and enhances the landscape, adding palm trees, native bushes, fruit trees and even orchids. Norma can name each and every one of the plants that grow on the property.

There is an interesting side note about the gardener, who came with his wife from the Czech Republic. After settling down, they bought a house, moved into the garage and rented out the house. Enterprising people these Czechs.

Walking around the grounds you will see at least three different banana tree types. There are also coconut palms, date palms, key lime trees and Jay's favorite, star fruit, all loaded and ready for picking. Jay says that back home a star fruit sells for a dollar or more at the supermarket.

In the Florida Keys it seems like everyone owns a boat and the Washabaughs are no exception. They own two and the larger one is named, *On the Rocks*. Fishing, of course, is a daily event with "Captain Tom," who has always been an avid hunter and fisherman. Captain Tom will take anyone out into the gulf and out into the ocean depths and they'll always come back with a catch. Jay and I had to throw our fish back because they were

Tom Washabaugh catches The Big One, Florida Keys

It's a Keeper. Meg in Florida Keys.

too small. But some one will always catch a few big fish for Tom to take home for dinner. Believe me no fish ever tastes as good as Tom's fish. Between Tom and Jay we have two great cooks in our Florida kitchen.

If you go on Captain Tom's fishing trek you'll pass a small island called Little Palm Island. It is accessible only by boat or sea-plane. Years ago it was a presiden tial retreat, but now it is a popular destination for the rich and famous. Just to dock your boat costs $262 a day. To rent a bunga-low costs $1000 per night and that doesn't include food or any thing else. Too rich for us!

Our granddaughter Jenny loves going out with her dad; while Julie prefers fishing in the canal since she suffers from motion sickness. What a relaxing pleasure to sit on the enclosed veranda or up on the sun deck watching the boats come and go. There is a "No Wake" sign at the end of the canal and once past it the boaters really rev it up. We sit and look for our Tom returning with the catch of the day. On one fishing trip the catch included a twenty-five pound tuna.

POWER SHOPPING AT WYNN DIXIE

There's nothing unusual about shopping to feed an army, and in our case, it's an army of seven. What is unusual about grocery shopping at the Wynn Dixie in this part of Florida is stepping out of your car and seeing chickens walking by, followed by baby chicks trailing behind mother hens. Wow, is this for real?

The shopping mall, which includes the Wynn Dixie, is swarming with them. They are known as "The Key Chickens" and they didn't always run loose. During The Great Depression, they provided fresh eggs and food for the few hundred people who kept them. With prosperity and the advent of food markets coming to the Keys the chickens were let loose and multiplied.

In Key West alone there are 2000 chickens. The island itself has only 25,000 people living on it. Attempts to send the chickens away to bird sanctuaries have failed. Key West is now considering hiring a bird catcher, or more appropriately a chicken-napper, at an annual cost of $20,000. Opposition to that idea is mounting and there is growing support to build a chicken sanctuary for the little critters right there, on Key West. Besides, chicken-napper opponents argue, they can't export the problem.

On the plus side, the free ranging Key Chickens are a tourist attraction which we all look forward to seeing each year. They also eat cockroaches, ants and even scorpions. They do a good job of attracting tourists and keep the pest population down, but the little battle lines have been drawn and we anxiously await the fate of the chickens.

KEY DEER

Big Pine Key is the only place in the world where you will find miniature deer. Standing less than three feet tall at maturity, the Key Deer is the smallest subspecies of the Virginia white tailed deer and is believed to have settled here from the mainland centuries ago. Classified as an endangered species, scientists at the National Key Deer Refuge have worked for the past 50 years to increase the population from only 500 to 700 deer.

Big Pine Key is now saturated with these deer and steps are under way to establish two additional herds just south of Big Pine, on Sugarloaf Key and Cudjoe Key. These two Keys are very small and can sustain about 40 deer on each.

Despite strictly enforced road speeds, road kill accounts for half the deer deaths. U. S. Highway 1 runs through Big Pine and is the only route through the Florida Keys. Highway 1 has been the target for a twelve million dollar project to prevent Key Deer deaths. Newly constructed fencing prevents the deer from crossing the highway, forcing them safely through an underpass to the other side. This has been an expensive, but successful, project.

We always drive slowly in hopes to catch a glimpse of the Key Deer and have managed to get some good pictures of the Bambilike creatures. But we always make sure to keep garbage cans covered and the gate at the end of the driveway closed as they love to feast on leftovers.

BACHIA HONDA STATE PARK

From mile marker 31, or Big Pine Key, travel northeast to mile marker 37 to reach Bachia Honda State Park. This 524-acre park has extensive sandy beaches and deep waters close enough off shore for snorkeling.

From a brochure at the park entrance we learned some interesting trivia about the park. Bachia Honda has many marine plants and animal species of Caribbean origin and one of the largest remaining stands of the threatened silver palm tree in the United States. The endangered small-flowered lily thorn can also be found growing on park grounds.

The geological formation of Bahia Honda is Key Largo limestone. It is derived from a prehistoric coral reef similar to the present day living reefs found along the Keys. Because of a drop in sea level several thousand years ago, portions of this ancient reef emerged from the sea, forming islands. Bahia Honda is the southernmost Key where this particular formation is found.

In more modern times, the park was part of Henry Flager's east coast railway holdings. The railroad was started in 1905 and was jokingly referred to as Flager's Folly. It was eventually completed in 1912 but later destroyed by a hurricane in 1935. The remnants of that railroad were converted into what is now U. S. Highway 1.

Cathy, Kayaking in Big Pine Key, Florida

KEY WEST

We have been to the Northern tip of the continental United States, the Keweenaw Peninsula in Michigan's Upper Peninsula. And now we have been to the southernmost part of the United States, Key West, Florida. Interestingly, both states share some claim to Ernest Hemingway. He spent days as a youth at the family summer home in Charlevoix, Michigan and he spent much of his later years in Key West.

In Michigan, Hemingway's summer home is a tourist attraction that has undergone a restoration. Included in the restoration is the outhouse which has a sign on the door which reads, "Hemingway sat here. "No doubt, this is true.

Key West Florida

Hemingway is everywhere in Key West including how so many men walking around look so much like him. Sloppy Joe's Bar on Duval Street in the heart of downtown, boasts that he frequented the place. There are pictures of him with the original owner of Sloppy Joe's and other important local dignitaries. Hemingway sat here too. When asked which chair; the waitresses will reply "take your pick."

Hemingway's home is on the main drag into downtown and is a tourist attraction. At $10 per person, people are lined up to take the house tour. What a gold mine.

Duval Street is filled with tacky tourist T-shirt shops, trendy shops featuring cigar-box purses, and saloons that advertise mojito magic hour. The Cuban influence is everywhere. Those who were able to escape Fidel Castro play a prominent role in continuing the Cuban tradition here in Key West.

You do not have to travel far for sight seeing. Among the nearby points of interest are:The original Pan American Airlines building. Pan Am brought the world its first international flight from Key West to Havana, Cuba, just 90 miles away.

The Audubon House and Tropical gardens on Whitehead Street is where John James Audubon stayed while painting wild life on the Florida Keys in 1812.

Father Tony, St. Peter Church, Big Pine Key, Florida

Discovery Undersea Tours 80 foot glass bottom boat offers a panoramic view of the reef and its colorful denizens. Key West Lighthouse Museum recounts Florida's lighthouse history. "Wreckers" is said to be the oldest home in South Florida.

Still bored? If you're out of things to do you can al ways find a bench and people watch. Various life styles are all on display here in Key West

ST. PETERS CHURCH

Mass at St. Peters is going to the dogs, literally. Father "Tony" Mullane's dogs make going to mass in the Florida Keys a unique experience. It begins before the service, with two dogs going up and down the aisle looking for head rubs. Then mass begins and the dogs join in the procession to the altar, where they sit quietly for the whole service. After Mass, they join the processional down the aisle to the front of the church.

Father Tony is from Ireland and is lucky to be able to return every year for a visit. He has had a quiet, but dynamic effect on the community. Be it the dogs or his service, Father Tony's congregation has grown and the church is being expanded to accommodate the increase in the Catholic Christian population in the area.

When I returned home I sent Father Tony a copy of my first book and he responded with the nicest of compliments. In a letter to me he said it brought back happy memories of his Irish roots. We hope to come back to the Keys and mass at St. Peters, God willing, as it is a most wonderful experience, especially at Christmas time.

God was willing, and we did return the following year, however changed.

MEDICAL HISTORY:
"THE GOOD LORD WASN'T READY"

My first battle with cancer was in 1990. I had ovarian cancer and I beat it. I thought that was the end of it, but in 2002 I learned I had breast cancer. That was devastating news for me as I was certain it would not show its dirty head again.

Having worked part time at Providence Hospital for 18-years I knew all the doctors there well and I was very comfortable with them. But by 2002, my doctors had moved out to Novi, which was an hour or more away. I was referred to a Dr. Ronald Vander Molen, a surgeon at St. Joseph's Hospital. He was one of the best things that could have happened in a bad situation. Dr. Vander Molen treated me with a great deal of respect, and in October of 2002, he preformed a lumpectomy which turned out to be cancerous. A few weeks later I had a mastectomy for a carcinoma in my right breast. Dr. Vander Molen had recommended that I have reconstruction at the same time as the mastectomy, but I was against it. At age 75, I thought "who needs that? "But I was wrong. Little did I know what negative feelings I would have each time I would look at that horrible incision area.

Technically, the mastectomy went well. When it was over, my respectful surgeon even said "it was a pleasure taking care of you. "But I was unhappy with my appearance and after months of looking at this awful mutilation, I changed my mind and decided to go ahead with a reconstruction.

NOTES FROM MY JOURNAL

March, 2003:I had the reconstruction done last week and already I feel good about it. I just returned from my first visit with my plastic surgeon. He removed my dressing and left the drainage in place.

I was worried four weeks ago. My mammogram showed an abnormality and I had to have another lumpectomy. Thank God it was negative for cancer.

"What an experience my hospital stay was. For two nights and three days I had a wonderful roommate. The hospital was understaffed on the weekend and because we were attached to so many tubes my roommate and I weren't much use to each other, we just couldn't help each other. Then my roommate's sister, a registered nurse, came to visit her. She was like manna from heaven for me as she helped me get to the bathroom by unplugging my equipment from the wall, removing my nasal oxygen, and pulling my IV after me. I was very weak and unable to do the normal things people can do when they're free of tubes.

The housekeeper went way beyond her duties to help me. She did things like put on my robe to cover my back when I went for a walk. She also noticed that my breakfast tray was in the wrong side of my bed and moved it over so I could reach it. She did similar things for my roommate.

My family wanted me to stay an extra night, as I still had a drainage tube in. When my wonderful daughter Margaret Mary saw how I emptied my bloody drainage tube she said "I do not do well with bloody bodily fluids. "I could tell by the negative expression on her face that she thought everything in the hospital was dirty. Shaking her hands she added "when I go home tonight the first thing I will do is take a shower. "My beloved husband is very similar to Meg but remained silent regarding his feelings.

On Saturday, the third day of my stay, all the IVs were discontinued and it felt great to be free. I was discharged on the same day and it was an RN named Pam who pushed me to the car in a wheel chair. I thought what a waist of an RN's time but apparently they don't have discharge transportation on the weekends.

When I finally got home all Jay said was 'I am drained' which is normal and to be expected after the many trips he'd taken back and forth to the hospital.

INTENSIVE CARE

My journal recalled that Jay was "drained" from taking so many trips back and forth to the hospital when I had my reconstruction. Unfortunately for all of us my stay in March was a breeze compared to what was coming.

I was admitted on July 1st with a fever and discharged July 6th. I was on home care IVs that consisted of an antibiotic which was clearly not helping to bring my temperature down. I was readmitted to St. Joseph's on July 11th after a visiting nurses aide discovered that I had a fever of almost 105 degrees.

Dr. Rula Mahayni met me in the emergency room and admitted me to the oncology floor for cellulitis, an inflammation in my right breast caused by infection. In other words, the breast implant used in my reconstruction got infected.

I was admitted on July 11th but I didn't come home again until August 27th. I spent five weeks and four days in the intensive care unit at St. Josephs Hospital. The only memories I have of the whole ordeal belong to my family. That's right I don't personally recall anything but the last four days. Everything

I know about those five weeks in ICU and just about everything that I am recounting here, I heard from my family.

When my fever didn't break and medications didn't work, Dr. Ali came into my hospital room at 9:30 PM on July 14th and announced he was going to remove the implant. On the operating table I went into cardiac arrest then a generalized toxemia shut down my organs completely. The hospital called Jay and then he contacted the girls.

The three of them rarely left the hospital, choosing to ride the roller coaster for five weeks rather than leave my bedside for very long. I had no idea that my great family would take it so badly, but it must have been hard looking at me on life support with all those tubes, a ventilator, a trachea and all sorts of monitors in me.

When Meg saw me for the first time on the ventilator, apparently she went berserk. She was skeptical about everything the doctors and shouted "holy so and so, they're not telling me the truth. "Of course they were telling the truth to the best of their ability. Meg was just so upset at seeing me in such bad shape. My nurse, Christine, had to tell her "if you continue to behave like that I will have to ask you to leave." Meg calmed down and she and Christine became great friends for the remainder of my stay.

Dr. Ann Washabaugh Matisse, our son-in-laws sister, was very helpful and emotionally supportive at this time. She worked as an interpreter or consultant for my family by explaining medical terms so everyone could understand my condition.

I'll always be grateful to her for her kindness, but when I bring it up Ann always says she was just paying us back for the kindness we showed her 13 years ago when she had brain surgery for a benign tumor and was then put on bed rest during her first pregnancy. She lived nearby and so Jay made sure she had enough food by delivering some of his famous cooking to her house. I guess what goes around really does come around, though I never looked at it that way.

My family came to see me in shifts. Meg took the evening shift, Jay came in the morning and Kit came in the afternoon, usually bringing along Jenny who was 10 at the time and Julie who was 12. Since they were too young to visit me in ICU, they stayed in the waiting room. Kit made sure they were occupied, so they were frequently busy knitting. Visitors were always so impressed to see these two young ladies patiently knitting scarves in the waiting room. The doctors asked them who taught them how to knit and they both would say "our grandmother, she is in there in ICU and we are waiting for her to wake up."

My family was so supportive, which impressed the hospital staff but also concerned them. My doctors worried about their health almost as much as they worried about mine. Jay was not eating well and he was losing weight and sleep. The girls were depressed. Kit just kept crying all the time and weeping "I just want my Mom back. "My doctor knew none of them could continue under all this pressure so he wrote them a prescription for sleeping pills and advised them to go home to rest, but they were reluctant to go, even my grand children. Jenny and Julie were busy knitting in the waiting room that day when Aunt Ann offered to take them to her house, but the children still said they wanted to be right there when Grandma woke up. It is in times like these that you really learn how lucky you are and I am very lucky to have such a devoted family.

Julie and Jenny Washabaugh. Too Hot to Handel concert

One day my son-in-law came into ICU when I was still on the respirator. I have always had a great relationship with Tom. He is an excellent father to my grandchildren, always willing to take the time to explain anything they want to know. On this day, he held my hand and asked, "How is the world's greatest Grandma doing? "Apparently I turned my head towards him and that was the first time I showed any reaction at all. The nurses were so excited.

Things finally began to turn around when I was given a blood transfusion. After three pints of blood and some changes in my treatment I finally woke up. My family was so relieved and overjoyed. They kept saying "we're so happy to have our Mom back. "Even now, when the children see me, they hold me tight. But imagine what a shock it was for me at the time to hear my children say "'Mom you were in a coma for five weeks and even the doctors did not know whether you would make it or not."

I know now that I was at a critical stage at one point and my family feared that they might have to make some life support decisions. I guess I didn't wake up a moment too soon. If the new treatment hadn't worked it may have been time to "pull the plug. "But the good Lord wasn't ready to take me and I am so thankful to have come out of it alive. I'm so lucky to be here today to enjoy my family and write about my miraculous return.

Cathy and Meg hiking in Ireland

After I woke up and they removed the trachea, I was able to talk when I held my finger over the hole. I kept repeating the same seven words "all I want is to go home. "It seemed like everyone ignored me, even my own family. It got to a point where I felt like they didn't even want me home. Then I heard Meg say to the doctor "we don't know what to do with her when we take her home."

I look back on it now and understand why they always shook their head and said no when I asked to go home. They were scared. They were afraid they wouldn't be able to take care of me. I couldn't walk and could barely talk. I had to write on a stupid small blackboard and my writing was so bad they couldn't always understand what I wanted. I remember one day I was so frustrated I threw the blackboard across the bed. Poor Meg was there to see it.

My children say the nurses were wonderful and never left me alone. They usually did everything in pairs and wore surgical gloves, especially when they had to change me like a baby. Since I was unconscious most of the time, I obviously can't remember most of them but I do remember a few of them. There was Mark, who was always very professional. There was Christine, of course, the one who became friends with Meg after she had to scold her to calm her down. I remember her asking me in a very low voice "do you not feel it when you have a bowel movement? "I said "why don't you offer me a commode and from there we can see what happens. "She laughed and from that point on I used the commode.

From the Intensive Care Unit, I was transferred to a room around the corner. I only stayed there for two days before I made the big move upstairs to the Rehabilitation Unit for daily physical therapy to help build my strength so I could walk again. After five weeks in bed, I was rather weak and unsteady on my feet. I took my first shower after I was moved up to the unit. The hot water running down my body was heaven.

The nurses and aides on the rehab floor were great, but extra cautious with me. I wasn't allowed to go to the bathroom by myself, even though it was just at the end of my bed. I broke that rule a couple of times and took matters into my own hands, but it upset the staff so I went back to being a "good" patient. I knew they were just taking the necessary precautions for someone who had just left ICU, but how I looked forward to Meg and Kit's visits. They helped me with all sorts of simple things that I couldn't do for myself, like getting to the bathroom. It was always more comfortable for me when they were there.

The rehabilitation staff was just wonderful, though at the time I complained they pushed me too hard, especially in the beginning. I didn't feel secure but as the days went by and I improved I began to trust the staff more and more.

Mark, one of the physical therapists, was a terrific person who also happened to be a slave driver. He encouraged me to work to my full potential, but at times I was so mad at him because I was convinced there was no way I could do it. But I always did and now I understand just how much I needed it. When I could stand on my own two feet I graduated to some more challenging exercises, like throwing a ball or walking on a treadmill.

I had many tests when I was in rehabilitation. One was a swallowing test. When I passed it they discontinued the IV and started me on soft foods like Jell-O, soup and a hi-nutrient drink. I still didn't have much of an appetite, nil to be exact, so it was a struggle to get anything down. Meg would look at my tray and say "Mom, you have to do better than this if you want to come home," but it had been almost two months since I'd eaten solid foods and I had to take it slowly.

I loved it when Meg and Kit would visit me. Kit came in the afternoon and Meg in the evening and I needed them both in the worst way. Meg would stand at the end of my bed with a lovely smile and that alone made my day. She'd help me brush my teeth and change into the clean clothes she brought for me to wear everyday. One day, bless her, she brought in some hair color and shampoo. Meg seemed to love to do my hair, even though there were times when I considered it to be nothing short of torture. It was amazing what the girls would think of and to my dying day I will be forever grateful to both of them.

What a joy it was to finally see Julie and Jenny. Even though they had come to the hospital often, they weren't allowed to see me because they were so young. I will never forget their lovely smiles when they saw me sitting up. We joked with Julie about someone pulling the tube out of my nose, but that wasn't true, I did it all on my own. Seeing those girls was some of the best medicine I received.

I remember two men, Matt a registered nurse and Eric, a male assistant. They would help move me when I needed it and often cleaned up after me when I was incontinent. They were a big part of the caring staff at the hospital. I thought Eric with his great smile would make a wonderful nurse and I encouraged him to go back to school to get his degree.

When I was ready to walk on my own, my doctors decided that with the additional help of a walker, I was strong enough to go home. That was my happiest day, the day my wonderful Jay came to take me home.

HOME AGAIN

We were in the midst of remodeling the house and on the day that I came home from the hospital the contractors were tearing down the garage. I was lying in bed and the whole house was shaking, but I did not mind. I was so happy to be out of St. Joe's and away from that hospital room. After seven weeks in a hospital bed it felt great to be able to navigate around my own home plus it was so exciting to see all the work the Amrael Build ing Company had done on the house.

When I first came home I had difficulty with sleeping, despite the painkillers and tranquilizers which did offer some relief. I was also clinically depressed, a side effect from some of the medication. Jay did his best to help me no matter what, but I still stayed up for a week with a bad case of insomnia.

I didn't have the energy of a flea when I got home, but I suppose that was to be expected after seven weeks in bed. Walking was horrible and it wasn't until after I was home that I finally began to understand why Meg kept saying in the hospital that I wasn't ready. I had no energy at all and I needed a lot of support.

Kit came whenever she could, but she lives about a hundred miles away so it wasn't easy for her. Meg, on the other hand, only lives about twenty minutes away so she came to visit every day. As a result, Meg soon became my rock and my right hand.

I had a kind and gentle physiotherapist named Cory who visited me at home three times a week for about five or six weeks. Cory developed an exercise program for me that included homework, like riding the stationary bike for twenty minutes on the days she wasn't here. She also had me exercise with bands which I found difficult. There were many times when I would rest and feel like I couldn't go on, but Cory reassured me that it was OK for me to do whatever I could.

A hospital social worker arranged for a nurses' aide to come twice a week to help me with my bath and a registered nurse came once every two weeks to take my vital signs and monitor my medications. All of my homecare was covered by our insurance. With a hospital bill of $209,000 we were all grateful to God for our insurance.

Everyday, I walked to the end of our street with Cory the physiotherapist, or Jay. In the beginning I was very weak and after only ten minutes I was exhausted. When I got to the last house I'd take a break and sit down to rest on the wall outside the home. One day, Steve, the homeowner came out of the house and offered to give me a chair, but I had to decline since Cory was with me and she only allowed me a couple of minutes to rest.

I started to do things on my own without the walker after about eight days. My appetite improved, which made Meg happy, and as my strength grew, I started to walk to the dead end of our street alone. Jay would join me later and we'd walk back home together.

Rackham Choir Fund Raiser dinner

When the day finally came that Meg bought me a bathtub chair and a special shower for the tub it was a big milestone for me. Suddenly I was capable of taking my own shower and dressing myself. I gained some independence and that was very encouraging.

In the cold weather I would try to remove myself from this house every other day. Sometimes Jay would drive me over to Somerset Mall where I'd walk for an hour. I'd get so tired I'd have to find a place to sit in the mall to rest every twenty minute or so. This was hard for me because I love walking and before my surgery I was very active. Growing up in Ireland I walked everywhere. We didn't have a car and the only other mode of transportation was a horse and trap. In the United States if I had a choice I'd always walk instead of ride. As my children always said, "Mom was born walking."

CONSTRUCTION PROGRESS

When the sun was shining, I enjoyed sitting in the back yard where I could watch the workers building our new garage, finishing the breezeway and working on the family room extension. We liked the guys who did the work, they did a great job and so we always kept them supplied with cold drinks during the hot weather and snacks when the weather changed.

I found the Amrael Building Company when I was walking my neighbor's dog. Since we lost Squeege, I missed the daily walks we took her on for fourteen and a half years so I asked the neighbor who lives three doors down if I could take her dog for a walk during the day while she was at work. She's a schoolteacher and was absolutely thrilled to let me do it. One day I walked the dog about a mile from here and came by a house that was having some work done. I asked one of the workers if I could have a business card, and he gave it to me. Then I spoke to the homeowner who just had a baby and she said to me "I will help you. I made about 18 phone calls before I finally decided on Amrael and now they are so good I gave them to my mother."

We hired them but because of my hospitalization, we had to put a hold on the project for a little while. After I came home from the hospital they really got to work and Jay kept calling me to say "Look how much they have progressed."

A girlfriend came to visit and asked me if we could move to the other side of the room because of the construction noise. I was amazed, we must have gotten used to it. I liked to call it a symphony, in that way I psychologically helped myself to put a positive spin on all the bang-bang.

Our house was built in the 1950s and this was the biggest project we had ever done. It was supposed to take about three months to complete the whole project, but my hospitalization, weather problems, the crew leader's medical problems and Birmingham inspectors put them behind schedule. I predicted that they wouldn't be done before Christmas and they weren't. They did a great job though and the new garage and sunroom make it look like a total new house.

Unfortunately the owner of the construction company went home to Israel for a week's vacation and while he was gone the crew boss got sick and had to be hospitalized. He is diabetic and they had to remove four of his toes. Eventually his leg was amputated above the knee. He's doing much better but when the owner returned from vacation he hired a new crew.

When all the bang-bang was finished we had to have some major plumbing work done so the bang-bang returned. But the bangbang beat didn't play for very long this time and we were left with a lovely new small white sink in the basement.

Finally we replaced all the bang-bang with piano music when we moved the piano by the window in the sunroom where it looks great and fits more comfortably. It's a Baldwin medium grand and it took up a lot of space in our living room.

It is so much fun to play the piano in the sunroom. I love to play, but my Jay is the more accomplished pianist and I've always wished that I could play as well as he does. He learned a lot from his father, the composer and professor of music who taught at St. Louis University and for whom the Becker College of Music is named. Meg brought me John Denver sheet music soon after I came home from the hospital because she knows I'm a fan and that's how "Sunshine On My Shoulder" was added to my repertoire.

MY PROGRESS

Two weeks after I returned home I was readmitted to the cardiac care unit of St. Joseph Hospital. I had never had heart problems in my life, but during the last surgery I did, so when I woke up at 2 AM with heart palpitations my doctor immediately admitted me into the hospital. We were all scared when I went back, but this time, I was only there for five days. They gave me a cardiac heart cauterization and thank God I didn't have any blocked arteries. I had a weak heart that wasn't pumping at its full capacity and my doctor put me on several medications to counteract it.

Back at home again there were times when I'd get really discouraged. I felt like I wasn't progressing as quickly as I should be. My energy level was so low and I would get so tired. I wasn't allowed to drive. Even when I was stronger my driving was still restricted to short distances because some of my medication caused drowsiness. But no matter how discouraged I got Dr. Vander Molen kept assuring me that I was doing great, considering what I'd been through. He warned me though, that it would take a good year for me to regain my strength and that just didn't seem fast enough for me.

I took ten medications every day. I tried to convince Dr. Vander Molen to discontinue some of them on several occasions, but he wouldn't do it. I have always been opposed to taking medications. As a registered nurse I gave medications out like candy and patients can become addicted to them. I had a couple of personal experiences where I watched patients sleep soundly after I'd given them a placebo. That was personally satisfying to see, but I rarely did it and I always informed the doctor before I did.

The medication I really hated was Tamoxifen. It is a horrible anti-breast cancer medication that made all of my hair fall out. I purchased a wig that I liked, but the girls didn't like it so Meg and a friend of hers took me to a wig shop and we bought another one that was more like my own hair color. So then I had two wigs that I liked, actually the truth is I didn't like them at all, in fact I hated them. But my doctor said I'd be taking tamoxifin for 5-6 years so I figured I'd better get used to it.

After my last hospital stay I had a wonderful visit from my dear friend Alice Moseley who lives in Arizona. Alice came over for the afternoon and we went to see a real good movie up town in Birmingham. The last time I saw her she was crying and rubbing my arm in the hospital. I was unable to speak and I was very weak.

Alice and I worked together for a closed head injury company in Detroit's Medical Center about 30 years ago. We were both nurse consultants and I really enjoyed the work. My duties included visiting closed head injury patients at home and in the hospital and arranging for their in-home medical care. The owner of the company had breast cancer, she passed away and the company closed.

Whenever I became discouraged it seemed something would happen to cheer me up, like Alice's visit did. I remember the first time I went back to the gym. I couldn't do a lot, but everyone welcomed me back with open arms. It was great to see all my friends at the aqua aerobics workout and the great welcome they gave me was a demonstration of how well I was liked, which was something I hadn't realized before. After the workout, my friend Maggie and I went to a nearby Coney Island and those people welcomed me back with open arms. What a great and happy feeling it gave me. It was times like these that gave me great hope and encouragement to move forward.

Linda Talacki, my aqua aerobics instructor encouraged me and helped me to build my strength by making sure I made it to class. She accomplished this by picking me up every Monday and Saturday morning to take me to the gym. In class, Cindy usually made me move with her, using extra continuous movements. After the class I dearly loved to follow it up with a 15-minute soak in the hot Jacuzzi.

Linda Talacki wasn't the only one at the health club who went out of her way to help me. The other members of the club were great too. One of the ladies who I met at the pool, Anita Mays, took me to a lecture.

Gilda's Club in Royal Oak was a tremendous source of support. I'd go every Thursday right after swimnastics, another swim class at the gym. Wonderful Diane from the St. Joseph's cancer support group in Pontiac introduced me to

Gilda's Club and even drove me to the meetings for awhile until I was able to get behind the wheel again.

At Gilda's Club I'd meet people who had really horrible stories to tell. Many had had a double mastectomy and other complications caused by cancer. It made me feel better to know that I wasn't alone and that I really was lucky to be alive. I appreciated the honesty that was expressed by Gilda's Club members. They were so open about their feelings and that made me comfortable talking about my own feelings, fears and frustrations. They were never critical and the group leader, Chris was a beautiful person who made sure no one was ever left out of the conversation.

In November of 2003, I started seeing a few patients and that also helped to improve my spirits. I'd only see one or two a week but that was about all I could physically handle. Psychological testing takes a total of six hours, but because I was still so weak, I'd do testing at two-hour intervals so that I wouldn't exhaust myself.

KEY WEST: MY JOURNAL, ONE YEAR LATER

A year ago I said I hoped to come back to the Florida Keys if God was willing. Thankfully he was.

December 2003: Today I started packing my own bags. I thank God that we are leaving for Florida this Thursday, December 25th.

We will be gone for nine days and since I've started writing my second book, I will bring it with me. Nobody has read it yet so I'll ask my girls and Jay to read it and give me some feedback.

It's nice to look out our window here in Michigan and see all the snow, but I prefer sunny weather. From the living room of the house on Big Pine Key you can watch the sunset. It is awesome. I also enjoy watching the boats going up the canal and out to the Gulf. It is so relaxing.

I'd like to go fishing alone with Tom this year so he can relax. He loves to fish but when he takes the others out he spends all his time putting the bait on their fishing lines. He doesn't complain. But if we went out on our own he could do most of the fishing and I would enjoy the quiet. But then again, I must remember to take it one day at a time.

January 2, 2004: We just returned home from spending nine days together at Tom's parent's home on Big Pine Key. Seven of us flew down there on Christmas day. We were there last Christmas, so I thought I'd be able to do the things I did last year. But a lot has happened since last year.

Last year we went to the beach, played tennis, rode bikes and I'd walk twice a day through the neighborhood admiring the nice homes. But that was last year. This year is different. I spent five weeks and three days in ICU at St Joseph Mercy Hospital and was discharged on August 27th. Doctors had attempted reconstruction of my right breast but when the implant got infected later, I developed generalized toxemia, all of my organs shut down and I was put on life support.

Last year we had such a good time. But this year I was too weak to do all of the things I did then. My family worried that I might overdo. Like when I wanted to ride the bicycle, Tom claimed he couldn't find the pump. That was his nice way of saying "no Grandma, I'm really scared you might fall."

When the family went to play tennis I wanted to go. What a mistake that was. I got sick on the field and Meg drove everyone home early. On the way back I vomited, but not in the car. I had only just asked Meg to stop and keep the door open so I could upchuck on the ground.

In the end, I spent much of my time in Florida relaxing with a book. I had company as Julie was engrossed in Harry Potter's latest adventure. I did get to go fishing with Tom like I planned and I really enjoyed it. We went out on his Dad's new boat and I caught two fish, but Tom would not let me keep them, he said they were too small. I always seem to catch the small ones.

Jay got to do what he likes best and lucky for me, that includes cooking. Jay loves to take a morning walk together and bring back the newspaper.

Jay and niece Pam Wilde. 2005

Kit and Tom have always been into fitness and the outdoors. She runs five to six miles every morning and has very healthy eating habits so it was no surprise when she and Meg decided to go kayaking through a mangrove forest. At $50 each for three hours, the adven ture begins in the over lapping National Key Deer Refuge and Great White Heron National Refuge on the back roads of Big Pine Island. Their guide, Bill Keogh, is their age.

As Bill leads the group, he tells them to go slowly to see more of the unusual ecosystem, baby snappers, tree crabs, herons, and egrets. They pass by No Name Key which has occupants but no electricity and a fabulous bar called the

No Name Key Bar which serves up the best pizza in the Keys. It is a popular tourist attraction because thousands of dollars in one dollar bills are hanging from the rafters and elsewhere. I recommend that you get there early or you'll wait a long time to be served.

Once past No Name Key, the adventure continues down the tree-covered mangrove. Meg and Kit report that the trip was an experience they will never forget, being so close to nature in the raw. Without question this will turn into an annual event for them.

On New Years Day we all went to mass at St. Peters' where I believe the parishioners are much friendlier than they are here in Detroit. Again, we saw Father Tony and his dog walk up the middle of church, pausing only so children could pet the dog on his way up the aisle. Last year he had two dogs walking up the aisle, and we took plenty of pictures, but this year there was only one dog. Father Tony's second dog passed away since our last visit.

Julie and Jenny kept themselves busy with their own activities. Little Jenny is a tomboy who loves to go fishing with her dad. Everyday they'd go out on the boat and come home for a swim in the canal at the end of the house.

Julie loves to read and as I said before she was glued to the latest Harry Potter book. She read it from cover to cover while we were there, all nine hundred and sixty pages. I asked her why she liked it so much and she informed me that it is so exciting since something different happens' everyday of Harry Potter's life. Jenny complains that she gets a headache when she reads too much, which I hope isn't anything to be concerned about.

Aunt Meg is extra close to the children and has been so since the day they were born. They are constantly asking her to play or take them to the store and she is always willing to give in to their agenda. Julie loves to shop, but not Jenny. Jenny would rather be fishing.

On the way back from Florida we were all separated on the plane, except for Jay and I, and that was only because a lady who had a window seat asked us to take it. We were delighted because that meant we could sit together. We have been flying on Northwest Airlines for many years and this time was the first time all seven of us were separated. It was also one of the few times that I flew without my knitting. Traditionally I take a book and my knitting along when I fly, but the strict rules imposed after September 11th won't allow me to carry on knitting needles anymore.

We left the Florida Keys about noon, and arrived back home at around 11pm. It was a long day but a great trip even if I couldn't do everything I did last year. I have to admit that at times it was trying time for me, but it was still great to go and great to come back.

MACKINAC ISLAND

Jay and I had planned to go to Mackinac Island in October 2003 with an

The view from the Grand Hotel over looking Mackinac Strait connecting Lakes Huron and Michigan

over 50's group called "Happy Travelers," but my medical condition prevented us from taking the trip. We had already paid for it and were resigned to the fact that we weren't going. But then we found out that despite her age, Meg could come as Jay's caregiver. So while they had some nice relaxing father daughter time on Mackinac Island, my dear friend Joan Bersani who I'd introduced to her late-husband Tony so long ago at Wayne State University, stayed with me as my personal caregiver for some nice relaxing girl time together.

The following year I was back in good health and got to go to Mackinac Island in October with Meg and Jay and the rest of the Happy Travelers. There are a lot of groups who go to Mackinac Is land each year but even after 16-years the Happy Travelers haven't been going the longest, another group has been going for more than 30 years. They may not be the longest running group, but they are certainly the largest group with more than fifty people taking the trip in 2004.

Everything is included in the trip, except lunch, which no one really misses. Our group organizer, Donna Jasin, has been doing this for several years and she's an outstanding planner, with movies, snacks and general banter the five-hour bus trip melts away. From the time you board the bus, stop for lunch, arrive at the ferry dock, land on the island and take a horse drawn carriage to The Grand Hotel, Donna's keen organizational skill are apparent everywhere.

There are 375 rooms at the hotel and no two are alike. We were assigned our rooms by draw, with the lucky ones getting a room with a Lake Huron view. The rest of us had a view of the heavily forested area in back of the hotel and in October that's not bad at all, the colors are breathtaking.

Everyone should stay at The Grand Hotel at least once in a lifetime. You won't be disappointed. The porch is the most famous and perhaps one of its biggest attractions. Said to be the world's longest front porch, it measures six hundred feet or is the length of two football fields. Built in 1887 by Senator Stockbridge, the hotel was sold to William Woodfill in 1919. In 1933, Dan Musser, nephew of Mr. Woodfill, joined in the operation of the hotel, eventually taking over as owner. The Musser family still owns and operates The Grand Hotel. Dan Musser, the third, is president.

A geranium theme runs throughout the hotel décor, and you see it everywhere, from the carpet to the stationery to the 1400 geraniums planted along the veranda. The variety is called "Yours Truly" and was selected for its large blooms.

Meg standing on the staircase of the Grand Hotel, Mackinac Island.

There are some 50 landscaped acres, 25 of which are intensively gardened. Each spring 110,000 plants, repre senting 105 varieties of flowers, are shipped from southern Michigan, trans ported by ferryboat and delivered to the hotel by horse and carriage. Why not by truck or car? In the early 1900s cars were banned from the island with the exception of emergency vehicles. So you have a choice. To get around Mackinac Island you can walk, bicycle, horseback ride or take a horse and carriage.

Speaking of a horse and carriage, the carriage tour is a must. There's so much to see from remarkable scenery to historical landmarks like Fort Mackinac, St. Anne's Church which is obviously Catholic because of the bingo sign, and the military cemetery where American and British soldiers who lost their lives in the War of 1812 are buried. Controlled by the French in the 1600's, the British held the island in the 1700's. The United States took over in 1783, but lost it to the British in 1812, only to regain it back in 1814. Mackinac Island is a treasure for any history buff.

Words cannot describe the five-star gourmet food served at The Grand Hotel. Breakfast is bountiful, and it's hard to imagine what else could be added to the menu. If you have room in your stomach, a full lunch or picnic lunch is also available, but not included with your room rate. For a real treat, try the elegant, traditional English afternoon tea. Finally, the Hotel's French head chef creates a five-course masterpiece evening dinner for up to 1400 guests. Fifty-two Jamaican waiters come to the island for the summer to serve meals in style with music emanating from the grand piano.

Grand Hotel, Mackinac Island

The Grand Hotel was featured in two Hollywood movies. In 1949, Xavier Cugat, Esther Williams and Jimmy Durante appeared in the film, *"This Time For Keeps."* The Esther Williams pool is still used today. Despite the fact that the pool is heated, Miss Williams still complained that the water was too cold and so the swimming scenes were filmed in Florida. This tidbit ranks among the worst kept secrets.

The other film was a romance called *"Somewhere In Time,"* that starred Christopher Reeve and Jane Seymour. It is a remarkable coincidence that we arrived on Mackinac Island on October 10, 2004, the same day that Christopher Reeve died. At the closing banquet of our Mackinac visit, Mr. Reeve, who was an activist for people with spinal cord injuries, was remembered in a moment of silence.

There are about five hundred people who live on the island all year round. Most of the resident's homes are in the middle of the island to block them from the winter winds off the lake. They most certainly must be a hearty lot.

In the winter, when the ferryboat stops and the lake freezes, an ice bridge forms between the island and the mainland. That's when snowmobile season begins. During this time of year the only way to bring people and supplies across is by snowmobile. For those who maintain the beautiful Victorian summer homes along the lake, the homes are boarded up to endure another harsh winter. A few summer residents and tourists come back for Christmas, but since many of the homes don't have central heating, I can only assume that a Mackinac Island Christmas is dependent on the weather report.

Jay and I at Grand Hotel, Mackinac Island

On our day of departure back to the mainland, Meg went power shopping. October marks the end of the tourist season and there are drastic markdowns in all the stores. Meg managed to finish some of her Christmas shopping in just a few minutes by concentrating on things which have Mackinac Island emblazoned on them.

Of course we didn't get to do everything we wanted to in the three days we were

Neil, Andrea McSweeny, Cathy, Meg and Margaret O'Sullivan at Jerry and Jenny's wedding

there. I am convinced that they do this on purpose to get you to come back to the island next year.

On the way back our tour bus stopped in Mount Pleasant for four hours of gambling at the Soaring Eagle Casino, which is operated by the Chippewa Indians. We chose instead to go visit a close friend and her husband who moved to the area from Detroit about three years ago. They said the casino had been a financial boon for the city, but for some of the Chippewa, the sudden wealth meant drugs and booze. We were sorry to hear this. When we got back to the casino we did gamble a bit and ended up $21 ahead, but we really don't care much for gambling.

THIS & THAT, PEOPLE & PETS

THANKSGIVING 2003

Both of my daughters took after their Dad the banker when it came to academics. Catherine Angela was always great in math, statistics and physics. Those were subjects that I was poor in and always tried to avoid.

Kit graduated from the Michigan Tech University with a degree in geological engineering and today works for the State of Michigan as a safety engineer. If there is an explosion in her area she is there doing an on-site inspection. She is on call 24-hours a day but is able to work from home.

She married Tom in 1983. They are very active, healthy eaters who take good care of themselves and their children. Tom loves hunting and fishing and Kit is a runner and a swimmer who shops at the Whole Foods store and uses a lot of fresh vegetables and tofu in her cooking. Jay has developed a taste for it and I must admit that I am learning to enjoy it too.

Traditionally, holidays are spent at our house, but in 2003 we had Thanksgiving at Kit's where the seven of us enjoyed their cooking of a very big bird. Everyone bought a dish to pass and in keeping with Kit's healthy eating habits we brought mainly vegetable dishes which tasted great. After dinner we all went to their Olympic sized swimming pool to swim off our feast. Tom's nieces joined us and so did his sister, Dr. Ann Washabaugh Matisse, who brought her two daughters with her.

There were about half a dozen children, between the ages of six and seven playing in the pool. They were all great swimmers, much better than I am. What a fun it was to watch them enjoy their swim.

Jay is a great cook and since he retired in 1989 he has taken over our kitchen. I remember when my sister Kate, RIP, came from Ireland to visit us. When she left to spend time with our other sister Joan in Virginia, Joan joked to Kate "there is no Jay in this house. "But now Jay was busy outside the kitchen as well inside. He kept up with the household duties with help from our cleaning lady, who came on Mondays. She was a Godsend as well since I couldn't do all the normal things I used to do around the house.

We also hired a gardener named Jack Mason. Jack comes every Tuesday and has really helped us out with the yard work and I love him. I met him at the park about 12 years ago when my grandchildren were toddlers playing on the

Shrine of St. Joseph Church, St. Louis Jay in front of cabinetry built by his great grand father Joseph Linkogel

swings in the playground. Chatting with Jack, I asked him if he would like to help us and if he would talk to my husband.

Jack has a degree in horticulture from Michigan State University and he's quite the character. He is a vegetarian who works in his bare feet. He has real long hair and a beard and doesn't believe in using electrical equipment. Jack won't even close the garage door because it's an electric door! And he once refused a ride home in the rain because he doesn't believe in cars, even though he was carrying home groceries. Jack lives like a pioneer and when he's working at our house, Jay always makes him a meatless lunch.

Hiring Jack was one of the best things I have ever done, not only for his work in the garden, but also because he transformed our basement into a workable area. Jay's workshop has never been so clean

BEAUTIFUL GRANDDAUGHTERS

I thank God for the many privileges I have had in living in this country with my wonderful husband of 48 years, and especially for my two great granddaughters and Julie Ann and Jennifer Reneé Washabaugh.

Julie was born on January 24, 1991 and Jenny was born on May 13, 1993. What a joy for me to be able to see Kit's daughters grow up and what fun it is to participate in their many activities and occasionally have them stay overnight at our house.

When the children were young we'd often take them for overnight visits. I adore them and when they'd stay I'd plan all sorts of adventures. We'd go everywhere. We'd go to Cranbrook and other muse ums, or the zoo, or the lake off Quarton Road to feed the wild geese. The more we fed the geese the more geese would come and I guess I thought the girls were kind of like that. The more places I'd take them too, I thought the more places they'd want to go. I was convinced that keeping them active would keep them happy. But I guess I over did it, so much so, that the children now say "Grandma, we do not have to go to all these places when we come down to your house. "What a big reality shock that was for me.

Julie & Jenny Washabaugh at The Hotel Europe in Kilarney, Ireland.

Both girls attend Faith Lutheran School up in Bay City, and both are doing very well in their academic studies, particularly math. Julie was promoted to a higher grade in math and Jenny came in first in a math pentathlon at their school.

My granddaughters are very athletic and into many sports. Soccer, baseball, tennis and swimming all keep them very busy, but like all true Beckers, they make time for music. Julie has taken flute lessons and both girls have taken piano lessons. Julie, taking after her great-grandfather, René Becker, has even composed her own music for the piano. I just love hearing them play.

Now that they're older and busy with school, sports and various other interests of their own, their schedules don't allow them to come down to visit me as much as they used too. So I go up there, to Bay City on Saginaw Bay, to see them. And you'll never hear me complain about it. Not only does it give me precious time with Jenny and Julie and Kit and Tom, but visiting their house is like going to a spa.

Jenny and Julie can usually find Grandma in their lovely heated swimming pool. It's an Olympic sized pool that feels like bath water. I use it frequently because water therapy is so good for my old arthritic bones. At home, I'm lucky to get to the pool two or three days a week at Kits I can easily spend about two or three hours in the pool everyday and the children often join me.

The children are great swimmers who had extensive swimming lessons when they installed the pool. Jenny has gone on to be a member of the swim team at school. But when we're in the pool together, I get upset if they stay under the water too long. I know they just do it to tease me because they laugh and say "Grandma you couldn't save us if anything happened."

Sometimes we go down to the beach. First we pack up the floats, rowboats and Libby, the dog, and then finally we're off. I swim out with the girls and when it gets to deep for me they pull my float and tie it to the stationary raft so I can get some sun and hang out with them while they swim and play ball. I love it when their friends join us. I think there are only two boys in their group and the rest are all girls. They play great together. Children have a unique way of making good friends. They can be total strangers one minute, then the next thing you know they're building castles and pulling one another in a row boat.

I have taught both girls to knit and presently they are both making scarves as Christmas presents for their friends. What a big pleasure it is for me to see them knitting. Julie is really into her knitting and says she loves it, but Jenny doesn't seem to be quite as keen on it as her big sister does. Of course that may change.

Jenny and Julie are beautiful well-rounded young ladies who appear self-contained and enjoy doing their own activities such as drawing, putting puzzles together and the like. A Grandma couldn't be prouder.

POEM BY JENNY WASHABAUGH

My school is a drag
No friends in sight
When I got myself into a fight
With a person who was always right
With a mouse in my hand I shook hers with mine
That was as she taught not very kind
And to make me understand that she had found it
She began to pound it
it ran up it ran down
Surely you think this took a lot of my time
But it really wasn't my idea
The secretary said my dear
And escorted her away
When I got home I checked the messages
Only to find a lot of questions
The next day I tried out for a movie part
The girl I tried to be was mean, sad and tart
Someone else got the part
And during the filming her room burned
As quick as a turn
she quit but thought I had something to do with it
And promised to ruin the rest of my life
I couldn't believe I had a part
But I would soon realize
It might be my last
I was right
A fire started and burned my sister
Bombs exploded, and smoke turned black
The studio was half gone
So I went home
To my surprise
I came back
And saw the same thing I saw before
Everything was back to normal
As I went inside I realized
That the wall was up and the paint was dry
I thought to myself and said they have so many people
For work that they almost don't need actors

when I had spare time I was looking for the culprit
By myself as I wondered was a woman smoking a cigar
I talked and walked with her into a barn
Where she locked me in a trailer, hit me on the head until she
thought I was dead
She threw her cigar in some hay
Thinking I would die today
But I found a red tool box with explosives inside
And blew up a door and was sent to a hospital
I didn't think it was possible
I recovered fast
And was told I wasn't aloud to go back to the set
But now I don't regret.

JULIE & JENNY & TORONTO

In 1995, we took Jenny and Julie to Toronto, Canada on the train and it was a trip I will never forget. Jenny was about four-years-old at the time and was still a dawdling toddler. Julie was six and off and running.

We stayed on the fourth floor of a downtown hotel. Julie, Jenny and I had left the room together on our way to the pool when Julie ran ahead into the elevator and the door closed before Jenny and I could get there. I ran as fast as I could back to our room with Jenny in tow to get Jay. Meanwhile an elderly lady riding on the elevator when Julie hopped-on escorted her to the front desk. At the front desk, Julie couldn't provide the concierge with much information since she only knew us as Grandma and Grandpa. She never needed to know our last name before.

Jay immediately flew downstairs and to his relief and grateful eyes saw Julie holding the elderly lady's hand. The concierge and the lady were both happy and relieved too when Julie shouted "There's Grandpa" and ran towards him. Jay thanked the lady and by the time Jenny and I made it downstairs everything had turned out fine. We went onto the pool as planned and our lovely little swimmers had a blast while Jay and I counted our blessings.

JULIE & JENNY & NIAGARA FALLS

Another big trip we took with our grandchildren was to Niagara Falls where we all went to the foot of the falls aboard the "Maid of the Mist. "We were three adults with two children who wanted to run from one end of the boat to the other. We adults spent all our time chasing after the kids to make sure they were safe.

We also took the girls to the Butterfly Science Center. There are signs everywhere that say "please do not touch the butterflies. "Jenny didn't have to touch one, one touched her! A pretty one landed on her finger and I was able to get a lovely picture of it before the attendant came and calmly shooed it away. Perhaps they should change the signs to read "please don't touch the people!"

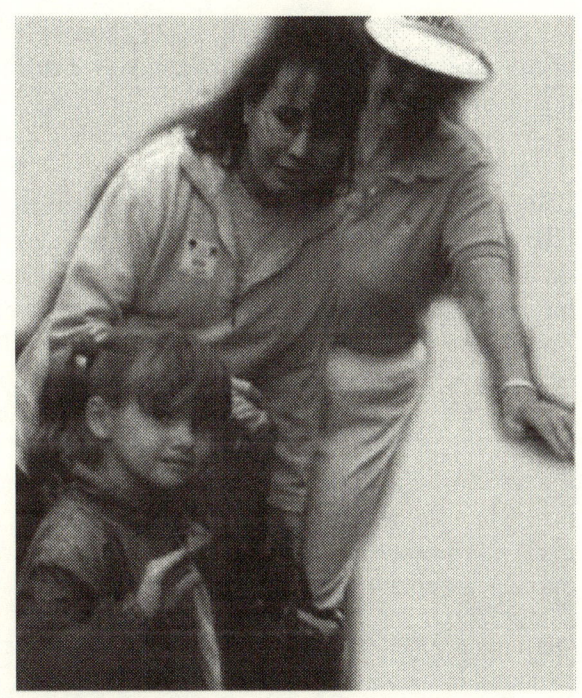

Niagara Falls, A butterfly lands on Jenny's hand

JULIE & JENNY & CHICAGO

Julie, Jenny, Aunt Meg, Jay and I went to Chicago on another trip. We took one of the last Pro-Jet flights out of City Airport. The company declared bankruptcy soon after. My nephew, Neil O'Driscoll met us at the airport and we stayed at the Courtyard Marriott in Arlington Heights.

It was a great trip. The hotel had a big pool for the kids. Neil's children, Maeve, 9, and Kate, 2, played well with Jenny and Julie. We took the children on the "El" to the Science Fair downtown and had lunch at the oldest restaurant in Chicago, a German restaurant called "The Berghoff. "I think the waiters were as old as the restaurant! They were well into there 80's, shuffling along and still providing first class service. Berghoff is also famous for being granted the first liquor license at the end of prohibition.

OTHER FRIENDS: ELIZABETH PAYDO & MAGGIE

Elizabeth Paydo is Meg's godmother. She lives in South Carolina now with her sister whose husband passed about six years ago. I met Elizabeth when I worked at Grace Hospital. She was the head nurse and was well liked by the doctors, patients, and staff. Elizabeth was instrumental in teaching the Irish nurses all the American rules of nursing. Always professional, Elizabeth certainly passed this quality on to everyone who worked with her.

Maggie is another close friend of mine. We like to meet at a family Coney Island restaurant where the food is home cooked and prices are reasonable. Like me, she was born in Ireland. She experienced hunger and cold, and like me, the pain a stern father inflicts on everyone around him. I don't know about hunger, I was raised on a farm and thankfully we always had plenty of food. But Maggie's father spent all his money on alcohol and there were times when he didn't have enough left over to even buy a loaf of bread.

Maggie's mother, sisters and brothers are all here in the United States. She will tell you that they all came over here for basic things like food, clothing and shelter which had been lacking back home. Her mom was in a severe car accident when she was still living in Ireland, but she was strong and was able to make a full recovery. Maggie vows she will never return to Ireland because of the accident that nearly killed her mother.

PRIVATE PRACTICE, PRIVATE PROMISE

I have been in private practice for about six years and have seen many wonderful patients. But one patient in particular inspired me to help her outside the office.

This patient was divorced with two children and her ex-husband was in jail. She had an associate's degree in mental health and I wanted to encourage her go beyond that. I promised her that if she went back to school and finished her degree, I would pay for it.

So she moved to New Mexico and enrolled at the University of Santa Fe, naming me as guaranteeing payment of over $900. I had completely forgot to tell Jay that I had made this promise to her and he found out about it at the worst possible time, when I was in the Intensive Care Unit at St. Joseph's Hospital. Jay thought this was all a mistake, but when another bill arrived he knew he had to investigate. He soon discovered that it wasn't a mistake and that the University was using a billing service to collect the money and that Jay had to send the money to them. Lessons learned!

They sent more bills and Jay eventually sent them some of the money, to the tune of $1000. But they wanted him to send it to an outside billing service and Jay wanted to send it directly to the University. After many phone calls and letters back and forth to the agency, he stopped sending any more money until I was back on my feet and could straighten out the whole mess.

What happened to my ex-patient? We helped her to get started and now she is in a position to finish herself. She has a full time job with benefits and is getting her degree on her own.

PETS

There are so many memories of Deputy Dog, our cream and grey colored mixed poodle who I wrote about in my first book. But I failed to mention our unforgettable visit with the Freeborough's in Lexington, Michigan. Lexington is a tourist town on the shores of Lake Huron. Deputy Dog was let loose and wondered off towards the lake when he decided to take a swim to Canada! Bad move, very bad move. The man who rescued him said he found Deputy swimming aimlessly in the lake, obviously disoriented.

Deputy Dog 1981

Squeege, another cream and grey mixed poodle came to us from Ed and Bea Washabaugh, grandparents of our son-in-law, Tom. Squeege was full grown and completely housebroken when she came to live with us in Birmingham. She had long legs, almost as long as her body and we learned early on that those long legs propelled her into a fast runner.

Just one block west of our home, our street, Pembroke, dead ends into a sort of mini park which houses a large water tank. We used to take Squeege out there on the leash and then let her go, and did she ever go. She'd take off like greased lighting around the park.

Now the city of Birmingham has a very aggressive animal control unit and we had to be ever mindful of the dogcatcher's schedule, but that didn't always prevent Squeege from wandering off through an open gate. One day we received a call from animal control that our Squeege was one of their guests and to pick her up. That was a 25-dollar lesson. A couple of times, Squeege, the escape artist would do an all-nighter checking out the neighborhood, but we always managed to get her back without police involvement.

Squeege went to dog heaven on July 4th 1999. Pet ownership taught us a valuable lesson, pets can be very expensive. Food, medicine and hospital care add up when you own an animal, and dogs and cats aren't tax deductible. So after Squeege died, we decided that we wouldn't get another dog. And that is how we started a new era in pet ownership with Willie, our pet betta fish.

Meg won a table prize at an office Christmas party and she gave it to us. It was a vase filled with water and a live plant. She was told that if she bought a betta fish it could exist on the plant roots. Not true. An internet search revealed that the fish needs additional food beyond munching on the roots of the plant. So soon after I bought Willie his diet improved with some much needed betta food.

We know our son Willie, the betta fish, is male by his rich blue coloring and fancy fins. All betta males are colorful with frilly fins, while the females are plain. Betta fish are a lot like birds in that regard, a male cardinal vibrant red and the female is a brownish color with some red.

Meg had a dog named Stroh's, which was the name of a local brewery. Stroh's, the brewery, was recently sold to Miller Brewery in Milwaukee. At one time Detroit was home to several breweries, but that sale marked the end of the last Detroit area brew houses.

Stroh's, the dog, was one half-Labrador, one half-terrier with a touch of bouvier. He was a funny, lovable mid-sized creature who always wore a red bandana. Meg doesn't agree, but Jay and I always thought he was a bit over-weight. We all loved Stroh's, the dog that is, and cried when he was put down.

Meg's attention turned to cats. We learned very soon that Meg could not pass up a stray cat. She had three of them. She picked up Spikes on a freeway, wandering about aimlessly. It turned out that Spikes was a cat's cat, which meant he became excited when he saw anything moving. A true mouser, if he saw birds or mice he was all meows until he was let loose to hunt down his intended victims.

Meg also had a cat named Jelly Bean, who was a phantom cat. We knew Jelly Bean existed because the food in her bowl would disappear, but we never saw her because she never ventured out from hiding.

Then there was Tykes, who was a birthday gift from her nieces Julie and Jenny. Tykes picked up some bad habits from Jelly Bean, but unlike Jelly Bean, he would come out for a visit to see us, but not before checking us out from a safe hiding place. Jelly Bean and Tykes were much more domesticated than Spikes, who couldn't wait to venture outdoors.

Kit and Tom have had a zoo full of animals at the insistence of my grand-daughters. Julie and Jenny's zoo has consisted of dogs, cats, hamsters, rabbits, Speedy the turtle (who was one of our favorites), and a whole lot of fish with a whole lot of bad luck.

They started out with a beautiful yellow Labrador named Angie, who loved to roam the neighborhood and had to be regularly retrieved home. Angie's workout regimen also included a six in the morning run with Kit through the neighborhood.

I loved the way the whole family prepared for her loss. They took final por-traits of Angie sitting on the front steps of their house. The children looked sad, petting her as they said their final farewells. They told her how much they loved her and would miss her.

Libby, which is short for Liberty, came next. She was another light yellow lab like Angie. And then there was Domino, a white and black cat who did more to disrupt family unity than any other creature. Domino was an outdoor cat, like Meg's Spike, lovable, at least from a distance. Domino was put out every evening and showed up every morning as if to say, "Hey, what's for breakfast?"

Meg of course, could not understand or tolerate Domino's dismissal from the house every night. So one day, she left the following note:

"Summary of the report to the Society for the Prevention of Cruelty to Animals Charge: neglect/abuse.

Arraignment date: March 22 2004. Judge: Roy Bean (The hanging Judge) Victim: Domino B. Washabaugh Details as follows:It is alleged that Dominos, hereafter know as 'the cat', is left to wander the streets of Bay City without supervision, from sunset to sunrise. It's not known who he is with or what type of activities he is engaged in. For all we know he could be out carousing or commiting crimes. He is also a suspect in a rash of cat burglaries. This type of behavior can only lead to a life of crime. It is recommended that the parents of the cat be enrolled in responsible parenting classes immediately.

Sincerely, a concerned citizen.
GOD BLESS AMERICA!"

THE PUMPKIN PARTY

We held the Fourth Annual Pumpkin Party at Becker's Acres on the first week-end of October in 2003. The highlight of the day is always watching the children as they pick out their pumpkins and discover the secrets of making honey.

St. Patrick's Day 2005, In Clearwater Beach Florida

Meg and Kit plan the party each year, sending out flyers and invitations and handling all the necessary arrangements, including renting a Porto John for our guests. Tom, Kit's husband, even brought down a stove so we could serve hot chocolate. And we always have a contingency plan in case of rain. The rain date is typically scheduled for the following day since we know we can use the pole barn for back-up if it's still a little wet the next day.

This year we were expecting between thirty and forty people. The official group picture shows 38 people, but we are sure there were more because so many people came and went all day long.

The week before the Pumpkin Party my kitchen in Birmingham is stuffed full of food, paper goods, and all sorts of other things ear marked for the farm. I'm always happy to see it all packed up and gone. This year I was particularly pleased to clear out the kitchen since I was still recovering from my hospital stay and I had very little room to walk around our small kitchen.

The girls went out to the farm early. I followed later that afternoon. I was surprised to see all the cars, but the biggest joy of the day for me was to watch all those darling children with their families picking pumpkins and smiling proudly as they packed them into their cars.

Some of the children went to the other end of our land to play baseball after they'd picked out their pumpkins. They were clearly having a great time since none of the children wanted to go home when it was time to leave.

It was great to see so many old friends. Our old neighbors from Detroit, Barbara and Dan O'Rourke, came along with a cake. Yolanda and Denis Delcotto who lived right next door to us in Detroit with their three adorable boys were also there. Both were great neighbors and we always had a great relationship, helping each other when we were needed. It really is nice that we are still in touch with them. So many others have passed on and I thank God for everyday I am alive.

My doctor's secretary, Amy, who has always been very kind to me, brought her two cute little boys and the children had a great time. Mother Amy was a little scared. The younger boy was a typical two year old who loves to explore and take chances. Our farm has lots of equipment which made her nervous, but none of it was turned on so it shouldn't be a problem.

Ken is the person Jay allows to use our ten acres to grow pumpkins and make honey. The main job for the honeybees is to pollinate the pumpkins, but the side benefit is the honey. Ken has four boxes of bees down by the barn. During the party, Meg and Kit will take some of the children there to show them how honey is made. But I always take time to warn the families with children that we have honeybees out there. That way they know to watch their children and keep them away from the barn unattended.

What a joy for Jay and I to see everyone, especially the children, having such a great time. We get so many thank you notes after the party telling us what a good time they had and reminding me not to forget to invite them again next year. And of course our granddaughters, Jenny and Julie, have made it very clear how much fun they have in Becker's Acres by pleading to us to "please never, ever sell the farm."

RACKHAM SYMPHONY CHOIR

Jay is very active in the Rackham Symphony Choir and has been the past twenty-five years. They practice every Tuesday for about two or three hours and once a year they have a dinner and silent auction to raise money for the choir.

I am always amazed at the wonderful articles people donate. Jay bought a lovely painting of a racehorse for $650. It was worth eleven hundred dollars and now hangs over my daughter Meg's fireplace. One year Jay took an old viola from our basement and had it restored. He also bought a new case for the viola, spending over $200. He donated it to the auction and it brought in $375 for an item valued at $500, which was a good deal for all sides. That same year I donated the proceeds from my own book *My Dream From Ireland To America.*

The Rackham Symphony Choir performed the traditional Handel's Messiah for many years at Old St. Mary's Church in Greektown and later at St. Peter and Paul Jesuit Church in downtown Detroit. In 2002, the choir premiered the jazz gospel version called *Too Hot Too Handel* at the Little Rock Baptist Church in Detroit to an overflow audience. With this success, the annual performance of *To Hot To Handel* is now held at the Detroit Opera House with Saturday evening and Sunday matinee performances. In addition to Detroit, Rackham will perform it in Chicago in 2005 and 2006.

From Detroit audiences we hear repeatedly "we were blown away with the music" and we're coming back next year. "I have to agree. I didn't think I would like it the first time, but it was just great. Watching the audience participate by singing and clapping with the music was so much fun to see. At the Alleluia the audience all stood up with thunderous applause and a standing ovation, clapping to the great music.

For me, the Messiah at the Detroit Opera House signals the beginning of our family holiday celebration. I am always so proud to see my beloved Jay, looking so handsome in his tuxedo, on stage with the rest of the one hundred-member choir. We gather for the concert and enjoy the Christmas lights, fine restaurants and other amenities downtown Detroit has to offer. Our newest favorite restaurant is "Small Plates" right across from the Opera House. We each order a couple of items to share with the rest of the family.

A MAJESTIC CELEBRATION

There were approximately two hundred guests at the Majestic Theatre that day in 2004 to celebrate Bob Van der Kloot's 90th birthday. Why celebrate his birthday at the Majestic Theatre? His parents were there attending the performance of a play when his mother went into labor and was rushed to nearby Grace Hospital where she delivered Bob. So this is where it all started, at the Majestic Theatre!

Bob's children planned a wonderful party and the food included Bob's favorite chicken. All the quests were invited up to the microphone to share stories about Bob. When I went up to say a few words, his daughter, Karen introduced me by telling everyone how

I took care of her when I was a nurse at St. Mary's Hospital in Livonia. She survived a serious accident on the freeway from Detroit to Ann Arbor and contrary to what is now said, had she been wearing a seatbelt she would have been killed as the car was totaled into a twisted mass of metal. Yes, this was an exception to the rule of always wearing your seatbelt. At the microphone, I shared the memories and concluded with a one liner from Bob Hope: "When you turn 90 you find that the candles cost more than the cake."

BILL & NORMA'S 50TH ANNIVERSARY

Kit's in-laws celebrated their 50th wedding anniversary in 2004. Tom video-taped the whole thing which was lucky for us since only the immediate family was invited and Kit was singing and we really wanted to hear her. It's a large immediate family, about seventy people, so we weren't insulted about not being invited.

Tom's sister, Ann, organized the whole event and did a first class job in getting everyone in the family to participate. Kit was asked to sing with Ann at the church, which worked out nicely. Kit has a great voice and Ann's is very powerful and together they blended beautifully. I loved it when both women invited the audience to join them in song by holding their hands out to the congregation. They put their heart and soul into the melodies and you would have thought that they had practiced a great deal, but I believe they only had a couple rehearsals.

Julie and Jenny had a role to play in the mass as well and I'm so proud of them. Julie did the readings clear as a bell and left the podium with such lovely dignity. Jenny and her cousin, Mary Matisse, were serving at mass. I wouldn't be surprised if Jenny was a little nervous since she'd never done it before, but if she was, it didn't show. I know her mother gave her a lot of encouragement beforehand. Jenny and Mary looked like true professionals as they cleared the altar.

Tom's 94-year-old grandmother was at the Church. She was in a wheelchair and I can only imagine just how happy it must have made her to see her son renewing his vows after fifty years. As for Bill and Norma, they looked so calm on the tape.

After church they went to a restaurant in Frankenmuth where the grandchildren urged their grandparents to re-enact their wedding vows. Their son, Jim, acted as priest and Norma even wore a veil as she walked up the isle with her grandson, Billy. This all took place in a private room at the restaurant to the delight of all the kids.

A year later and we're still blown away by that wonderful service. I am so happy that my great son-in-law videotaped everything to share with us. I will be eternally grateful to him for so many things.

AN IRISH WEDDING

My nephew, Jerry Kelleher was married on Thursday, September 30th 2004, at Ballintubber Abbey in County Mayo. The abbey was built in 1216. Meg and Kit went, but Jay and I did not

Jerry and Jenny Kelleher's wedding, County Mayo, Sept. 30, 2004

attend. But it felt like we were there because Meg took a camcorder so we could see the wedding on video.

The brides maids were Orla Flannery and Rosemary Kelleher, and the Celebrants were Father Gerry O'Hora and Father James McSweeney. The readers were Jim Browne and Rosemary Kelleher. Prayers of the faithful were read by Ann Farrell and Ursula Coffey. The wonderful soloist was Sharon Aris. She sang a very powerful *Ave Maria* (Franz Schubert) and *Panis Angelicus* (C. Franck) that left a lasting impression on the congregation. And at the end of the service, my nephew Patrick O' Driscoll, played his Irish bagpipes for the happy couple as they left the abbey.

That evening, after the service there was a big party at the Westport Hotel. What fun for me to see and hear my whole family singing and dancing Irish songs that were so familiar to me, like *When Irish Eyes Are Smiling* and *I Will Take You Home Again Kathleen.* My brother Patsy, who lives in California, was dancing with Kit who wore a lovely pink shawl, and every time my brother twirled my daughter around that pink shawl flew out delightfully.

Meg was busy taking the pictures until someone took over for her and she was able to talk to us on the tape. She ended by pointing her thumb upwards and said "over and out" just like an overseas correspondent.

Descending Clara Mountain, Millstreet

FINAL THOUGHTS

Our names appear on a genealogy chart or family tree along with many other names. Who are we? Who are they? In many, if not most cases, we know very little about each other. My first book, **_My Dream From Ireland To America_** inspired more than one person to sit down and write things to pass on to their families. This new book continues where my first book left off, my own reflections through vignettes a message of love and togetherness. The love was never so strong or evident as it was in 2003 when I fought to stay alive. Those memories are preserved here in this book to pass on to our grandchildren's children.

My personal thanks to Leona Gould-McElhone whose writing skills kept me on a straight and narrow path as she prodded me not to write this book like a diary but as a collection of memories and stories to pass onto family, friends, and future generations. Thanks to my immediate family and friends as well, who guided me down memory lane. And with that I say TTFN, Ta-Ta for now.

P.S.

I walked daily through the fields at the back of our house and it was during one of my many walks that I met wonderful Donna Sullivan. She was and continues to be an inspiration to me. Donna is a classy lady who encouraged me to keep writing.

Mary Ann Molner who survived breast cancer is related to my husband as their grand mothers were sisters. Ever since finding this out we have become fast friends and share loving moments together. A superb genealogist, we are thankful that she took the time to track us down.

A retired C.P.A. whose avocation is music, Richard Mervyn Cooper from Ireland contacted my husband concerning the music of Rene and Angela

Becker after recently reading the American Organist article about them. He now promotes their music in Dublin. Thank you Mervyn.

    ∾ A special thanks to *Dr. Sholeh Vaziri* who saved my life and continues to watch over me.

978-0-595-38318-4
0-595-38318-1

www.ingramcontent.com/pod-product-compliance
Lightning Source LLC
Chambersburg PA
CBHW020430290526
45785CB00002B/782